EXAMINING SIMILARITIES & DIFFERENCES

CLASSROOM TECHNIQUES TO HELP STUDENTS DEEPEN THEIR UNDERSTANDING

EXAMINING SIMILARITIES & DIFFERENCES

CLASSROOM TECHNIQUES TO HELP STUDENTS DEEPEN THEIR UNDERSTANDING

Connie Scoles West and Robert J. Marzano

With Kathy Marx and Penny L. Sell

LearningSciences
MARZANO
CENTER

1400 Centrepark Blvd, Suite 1000
West Palm Beach, FL 33401
717-845-6300

email: pub@learningsciences.com
learningsciences.com

Printed in the United States of America

20 19 18 17 16 15   2 3 4

Publisher's Cataloging-in-Publication Data

Scoles West, Connie.
  Examining similarities & differences : classroom techniques to help students deepen their understanding / Connie Scoles West [and] Robert J. Marzano.
    pages cm. – (Essentials for achieving rigor series)
  ISBN: 978-1-941112-05-2 (pbk.)
1. Thought and thinking—Study and teaching. 2. Critical thinking—Study and teaching. 3. Effective teaching—United States. 4. Metaphor. 5. Analogy. I. Marzano, Robert J. II. Title.
  LB1060 .S383 2015
  370.15—dc23
                          [2014939270]

MARZANO CENTER

Essentials for Achieving Rigor SERIES

The *Essentials for Achieving Rigor* series of instructional guides helps educators become highly skilled at implementing, monitoring, and adapting instruction. Put it to practical use immediately, adopting day-to-day examples as models for application in your own classroom.

Books in the series:

Identifying Critical Content: Classroom Techniques to Help Students Know What Is Important

Examining Reasoning: Classroom Techniques to Help Students Produce and Defend Claims

Recording & Representing Knowledge: Classroom Techniques to Help Students Accurately Organize and Summarize Content

Examining Similarities & Differences: Classroom Techniques to Help Students Deepen Their Understanding

Processing New Information: Classroom Techniques to Help Students Engage with Content

Revising Knowledge: Classroom Techniques to Help Students Examine Their Deeper Understanding

Practicing Skills, Strategies & Processes: Classroom Techniques to Help Students Develop Proficiency

Engaging in Cognitively Complex Tasks: Classroom Techniques to Help Students Generate & Test Hypotheses across Disciplines

Using Learning Goals & Performance Scales: How Teachers Make Better Instructional Decisions

Organizing for Learning: Classroom Techniques to Help Students Interact within Small Groups

Table of Contents

Acknowledgments

I would like to thank my colleagues from Learning Sciences International who have done so much to provide guidance and opportunities. Many thanks to Michael Toth, Bryan Toth, and Beverly Carbaugh, and to my fellow staff developers who are a constant source of help and support for me.

In addition, I must recognize all the wonderful school administrators and teachers who have been participants in my sessions. They are the source of many of the ideas and examples in this book. Finally, I want to acknowledge Paul West, extraordinary teacher and husband, who patiently listens, shares, serves as a sounding board, and always supports.

—Connie Scolcs West

Learning Sciences International would like to thank the following reviewers:

Kristi Bundy
2014 Nebraska Teacher of the Year
Ashland-Greenwood Public Schools
Ashland, Nebraska

Jennie Dearani Calnan
2014 New Hampshire Teacher of the
   Year finalist
District Literacy Plan Coordinator
Reading Specialist
Monadnock Regional School District
Swanzey, New Hampshire

Maureen Look
2011 Wisconsin Teacher of the Year
Eighth-Grade Science and
   Engineering Educator
Milwaukee, Wisconsin

Jamie Manker
2014 Missouri Teacher of the Year
Rockwood Summit High School
Fenton, Missouri

Barbara Rosolino
2013 Georgia Teacher of the Year
   finalist
Eagle's Landing High School
McDonough, Georgia

Tracie Wagenfeld
2014 Maine Teacher of the Year
   finalist
Fifth-Grade Teacher
Willard School
Sanford, Maine

About the Authors

CONNIE SCOLES WEST, BSEd, MEd, spent her career in K–12 education as a classroom teacher and administrator in Cincinnati, Ohio, before joining Learning Sciences International as an independent staff developer in 2012. Connie brings expertise to her work from years of experience in a broad spectrum of leadership roles, including gifted education, mentoring, instructional coaching, school improvement, curriculum, professional development, and teacher evaluation. She has presented at numerous conferences on topics in literacy, mathematics, coaching, and curriculum and instruction. Connie earned bachelor's and master's degrees in education from Miami University in Oxford, Ohio.

ROBERT J. MARZANO, PhD, is CEO of Marzano Research Laboratory and Executive Director of the Learning Sciences Marzano Center for Teacher and Leader Evaluation. A leading researcher in education, he is a speaker, trainer, and author of more than 150 articles on topics such as instruction, assessment, writing and implementing standards, cognition, effective leadership, and school intervention. He has authored over 30 books, including *The Art and Science of Teaching* (ASCD, 2007) and *Teacher Evaluation That Makes a Difference* (ASCD, 2013).

KATHLEEN MARX, MSEd (Educational Leadership), MSEd (School Counseling), is a leading expert in personal development across industries. She has successfully assisted many districts nationally to implement deep school-improvement changes through her work with Learning Sciences International.

PENNY SELL, MSEd, has spent more than 30 years in public education, and her roles have included teacher, administrator, trainer, and consultant. She earned her bachelor's degree in exceptional education from Central Michigan University and master's degree in educational leadership from the University of Central Florida.

Introduction

This guide, *Examining Similarities & Differences: Classroom Techniques to Help Students Deepen Their Understanding,* is intended as a resource for improving a specific strategy of instructional practice: examining similarities and differences.

Your motivation to incorporate this strategy into your instructional toolbox may have come from a personal desire to improve your instructional practice through the implementation of a research-based set of strategies (such as those found in the Marzano instructional framework) or a desire to increase the rigor of the instructional strategies you implement in your classroom so that students meet the expectations of demanding standards such as the Common Core State Standards, Next Generation Science Standards, C3 Framework for Social Studies State Standards, or state standards based on or influenced by College and Career Readiness Anchor Standards.

This guide will help teachers of all grade levels and subjects improve their performance of a single instructional strategy: examing similarities and differences. Narrowing your focus on a specific skill, such as examining similarities and differences, will enable you to more fully understand its complexities to intentionally improve your instruction. Armed with deeper knowledge and practical instructional techniques, you will be able to intentionally plan, implement, monitor, adapt, reflect, and ultimately improve upon the execution of this element of your instructional practice. An individual seeking to become an expert displays distinctive behaviors, as explained by Marzano and Toth (2013):

- breaks down the specific skills required to be an expert

- focuses on improving those particular critical skill chunks (as opposed to easy tasks) during practice or day-to-day activities

- receives immediate, specific, and actionable feedback, particularly from a more experienced coach

- continually practices each critical skill at more challenging levels with the intention of mastering it, giving far less time to skills already mastered

This series of guides will support each of the previously listed behaviors, with a focus on breaking down the specific skills required to be an expert and giving day-to-day practical suggestions to enhance these skills.

Building on the Marzano Instructional Model

This series is based on the Marzano instructional framework, which is grounded in research and provides educators with the tools they need to connect instructional practice to student achievement. The series uses key terms that are specific to the Marzano model of instruction. See Table 1, Glossary of Key Terms.

Table 1: Glossary of Key Terms

Term	Definition
CCSS	Common Core State Standards is the official name of the standards documents developed by the Common Core State Standards Initiative (CCSSI), the goal of which is to prepare America's students for college and career.
CCR	College and Career Readiness Anchor Standards are broad statements that incorporate individual standards for various grade levels and specific content areas.
Desired result	The intended result for the student(s) due to the implementation of a specific strategy.
Monitoring	The act of checking for evidence of the desired result of a specific strategy while the strategy is being implemented.
Instructional strategy	A category of techniques used for classroom instruction that has been proven to have a high probability of enhancing student achievement.
Instructional technique	The method used to teach and deepen understanding of knowledge and skills.
Content	The knowledge and skills necessary for students to demonstrate standards.
Scaffolding	A purposeful progression of support that targets cognitive complexity and student autonomy to reach rigor.
Extending	Activities that move students who have already demonstrated the desired result to a higher level of understanding.

The educational pendulum swings widely from decade to decade. Educators move back and forth between prescriptive checklists and step-by-step lesson plans to approaches that encourage instructional autonomy with minimal regard for the science of teaching and need for accountability. Two practices are often missing in both of these approaches to defining effective instruction: 1) specific statements of desired results, and 2) solid research-based connections. The Marzano instructional framework provides a comprehensive system that details what is required from teachers to develop their craft using research-based instructional strategies. Launching from this solid instructional foundation, teachers will then be prepared to merge that science with their own unique, yet effective, instructional style, which is the art of teaching.

Examining Similarities & Differences: Classroom Techniques to Help Students Deepen Their Understanding will help you grow into an innovative and highly skilled teacher who is able to implement, scaffold, and extend instruction to meet a range of student needs.

Essentials for Achieving Rigor

This series of guides details essential classroom strategies to support the complex shifts in teaching that are necessary for an environment where academic rigor is a requirement for all students. The instructional strategies presented in this series are essential to effectively teach the CCSS, the Next Generation Science Standards, or standards designated by your school district or state. They require a deeper understanding, more effective use of strategies, and greater frequency of implementation for your students to demonstrate the knowledge and skills required by rigorous standards. This series includes instructional techniques appropriate for all grade levels and content areas. The examples contained within are grade-level specific and should serve as models and launching points for application in your own classroom.

Your skillful implementation of these strategies is essential to your students' mastery of the CCSS or other rigorous standards, no matter the grade level or subject matter you are teaching. Other instructional strategies covered in the Essentials for Achieving Rigor series, such as examining reasoning and engaging students in cognitively complex tasks, exemplify the cognitive complexity needed to meet rigorous standards. Taken as a package, these strategies may at first glance seem quite daunting. For this reason, the series focuses on just one strategy in each guide.

Examining Similarities and Differences

The topic of this guide, examining similarities and differences, is an instructional strategy comprising four discrete cognitive processes: comparing, classifying, creating metaphors, and creating analogies. Each of these processes, when directly taught to and modeled for students, has the potential not only to deepen their understanding of content knowledge but also enhance their long-term retention and problem-solving abilities related to critical content. A simple way to think about this strategy is to recall a song from the *Sesame Street* TV show: "One of these things is not like the others." That song is based on a cognitive process critical to the acquisition of knowledge: identifying the basic relationships between objects, ideas, concepts, events, places, and people.

Your students' abilities to interact with content while processing that content by comparing, classifying, and creating metaphors or analogies enables them to constantly add new content knowledge to previously learned material in their long-term memories, thereby creating new and deeper knowledge. The purpose of this guide is to give you specific techniques to teach your students how to examine similarities and differences in the context of critical content.

The Effective Implementation of Examining Similarities and Differences

There are six steps that will lead you to the effective implementation of examining similarities and differences:

1. Develop and consistently use student-friendly definitions for the four cognitive processes that comprise examining similarities and differences: 1) comparing, 2) classifying, 3) creating metaphors, and 4) creating analogies.

2. Directly teach and intentionally model these four cognitive processes for students.

3. Gain proficiency in teaching and modeling the mental tools students need to examine similarities and differences as they pertain to critical content: 1) identifying critical attributes, 2) summarizing, and 3) generalizing.

4. Gain proficiency in teaching and modeling the recording and representing tools students need to examine similarities and differences as they pertain to critical content: 1) sentence stems and 2) graphic organizers.

5. Continually remain focused on student mastery of critical content as the ultimate goal of examining similarities and differences.

6. Gradually release responsibility to students for managing their own thinking and learning about the similarities and differences in critical content.

Each of these six prerequisites is described in more detail in the following sections. First, think about what you already know and understand about identifying similarities and differences. Then, integrate any new information that expands and enriches your previous understandings.

Master the Definitions

As an educator, you have no doubt routinely used the terms *compare, classify, metaphor,* and *analogy* in your own academic endeavors as well as your classroom. However, to successfully implement examining similarities and differences, you will need to develop solid student-friendly definitions for these terms. In addition, you will need to develop a comprehensive understanding of how the demands of your content and the background knowledge and maturity of your students interact with these processes.

Collaborate with colleagues on writing common definitions, and use the following definitions to anchor your implementation. The words in parentheses are synonyms that are appropriate for use with older learners. However, if you teach primary students, keep the definitions simple and student friendly.

- *Comparing* is a way (a cognitive process) to identify similarities and differences between or among things.

- *Classifying* is a way to put things that are alike into categories based on their characteristics (attributes, properties, traits).

- A *metaphor* is a characteristic (attribute) shared by two objects (topics) that seem to be quite different.

- An *analogy* is a comparison of two similar objects (things, ideas, people).

Notice that the first two terms (*comparing* and *classifying*) are cognitive processes and the last two terms (*metaphor* and *analogy*) are patterns that communicate relationships between things. To create metaphors and analogies based on content, students must be able to identify similarities and differences. Also recall that the term *comparing* used in the context of this guide carries the meaning of both comparing *and* contrasting.

Directly Teach and Intentionally Model

If your students are to become skilled at cognitively processing content as just described, first directly teach them what an individual process is and what kinds of thinking demands are required to execute the process. Then, be prepared to think aloud and model for them how and what you are thinking as you examine similarities and differences. This kind of modeling requires that you intentionally slow down your own thinking in order to articulate for students the kinds of connections, background knowledge, and problem solving you are drawing upon to make sense of the similarities and differences in the content or text.

Gain Proficiency Using the Mental Tools Needed to Examine Similarities and Differences

There are three mental tools that will frequently be mentioned in the context of effectively implementing examining similarities and differences: 1) identifying critical attributes, 2) summarizing, and 3) generalizing. The first tool comes into play the minute you decide to use a comparing or classifying technique. Unless both you and your students understand and can identify the important characteristics or attributes of the two or more things that will be compared or classified, you will be wasting precious instructional time on unimportant information. You should routinely use either of the other tools—summarizing and generalizing—to conclude any lesson in which students have identified similarities and differences.

Gain Proficiency Using the Recording and Representing Tools Needed to Examine Similarities and Differences

In addition to the mental tools described previously, there are two tools for recording and representing that will enhance your students' abilities to understand and remember critical content: 1) sentence stems and 2) graphic organizers. Sentence stems are sentence skeletons that contain a basic structure setting forth the parameters of a thinking task combined with blanks for students to fill in with appropriate answers. Sentence stems can be used for comparing tasks as well as creating analogies and metaphors.

Graphic organizers are another important tool for representing similarities and differences. There are specific organizers for both comparing and classifying. Note that graphic organizers and sentence stems are means to the end (examining similarities and differences)—not ends in and of themselves. Sentence stems and/or organizers are found throughout this guide. In addition, templates for many of the organizers are found in Resource A.

Focus on Content

No matter which technique you choose for teaching examining similarities and differences to your students, remain focused on content. Content goals often involve both *declarative knowledge* (informational) and *procedural knowledge* (skills and processes). The strategy presented in this guide is most effective in helping students deepen their understanding of declarative knowledge. The strategy can also clarify confusion between related concepts. Examining similarities and differences is applicable to all disciplines and grade levels.

As you become more skilled in applying this strategy, you will see remarkable changes in your students' abilities to process and understand content. They will be able to generalize and refine schema independently. You can effectively implement this strategy by engaging students in the many different instructional techniques found in this guide.

Gradually Release Responsibility for Thinking to Students

You can easily lose sight of your defining role as a teacher: getting your students ready to assume total responsibility for their own thinking about similarities and differences. Expecting students to copy your notes and graphic organizers from the board and dictating to students how their sentence stems should be completed are two powerful ways to undermine and diminish your students' opportunities to learn.

The following teacher behaviors are associated with the effective implementation of examining similarities and differences:

- identifying critical content for examination

- identifying the similarities and differences between critical content concepts

- providing opportunities for students to linguistically and nonlinguistically represent similarities and differences

- asking students to summarize what they have learned from a lesson or text

- guiding students to generalize or draw conclusions after the examination of similarities and differences

- facilitating the use of digital resources to find credible and relevant information to support the examination of similarities and differences

As you set out to become more skilled at implementing this strategy, think about how you can avoid some of the common mistakes. The following roadblocks can very quickly take your teaching and students' learning off course:

- The teacher fails to take the time needed to directly teach and model the strategy.

- The teacher fails to facilitate his students' abilities to identify critical attributes specifically related to critical content.

- The teacher fails to take into account students' background knowledge and working memory capacities by asking them to compare too many things using too many comparison criteria.

- The teacher fails to ask students to draw conclusions or make generalizations after a lesson, depriving them of the most important aspect of this strategy.

Failing to Take the Time Needed

When students examine similarities and differences, they are asked to analyze specific topics based on certain criteria to gain new insights and come to deeper understandings. To do this well, students first must have some foundational knowledge about each thing being compared. If they know little, or have only superficial basic knowledge, then the activity will not be of much benefit. Provide students adequate time and learning experiences to understand foundational information before asking them to examine similarities and differences.

Failing to Consider Students' Readiness for the Task

Although it is tempting to add more topics to compare, or list more criteria to examine, beware of creating a task that is too complicated for students to complete well. Choose a reasonable number of topics to compare (typically two or three) with a small number of important criteria to look at for each topic.

Failing to Consider Students' Background Knowledge

A common mistake related to students' readiness is overlooking how much you know about a topic in comparison to what your students know. Bear in mind that any lesson that assumes your students have background knowledge they do not is destined to end in frustration for both you and your students.

Failing to Generalize Findings

The intended outcome of comparison activities is for your students to gain new insight into the content. Expect students to generalize and summarize their findings as a final step in any lesson. Without this final step, students may exit your classroom without the kind of deep and long-lasting knowledge they need to succeed at the next level.

Monitoring for the Desired Result

An instructional strategy is only as effective as the learning that results from its implementation. Effective implementation of this strategy is more than just having students participate in a thought-provoking or engaging activity. It must include monitoring. Ask: *Did my students deepen their understanding of the content by completing this work? How do I find out?* In fact, consider a more specific question: *Was the desired result of the strategy achieved?*

Specifically, the desired result of examining similarities and differences is for students to be able to describe how various aspects of the content are similar and different and then be able to state any new information or generalizations they have learned as a result of the activity. There are multiple ways teachers can monitor whether the majority of students are displaying this desired result:

1. Students can create analogies and/or metaphors that reflect their depth of understanding of content.

2. Students' comparison and classification activities reflect their depth of understanding of content.

3. Students' work indicates that they have accurately identified similarities and differences and can show how their knowledge has been extended as a result of the activity.

4. Students can summarize their findings relative to examining similarities and differences.

5. Students can present evidence to support their explanation of similarities and differences.

6. Students can generalize patterns or draw conclusions about insights gained and apply them to new examples and ideas.

7. Students can navigate digital resources to find credible and relevant information to support similarities and differences.

Because this strategy—*examining similarities and differences*—requires deep and rigorous thinking, monitoring will require that you ask probing questions, assess the quality of group discussions and student work, and observe students closely during the lesson. Find ways to hear the thinking of each student, and do not accept group responses as an effective means of monitoring individuals. In addition, give students opportunities to revise their thinking after a lesson or discussion and to also explain how they gained a better understanding of the important content. This broader and deeper understanding of monitoring will strengthen and improve your teaching performance and ultimately your students' learning.

Scaffolding and Extending Instruction to Meet Students' Needs

As you monitor for the desired result of this strategy, you will probably realize that some students are not able to accurately identify similarities and differences or generalize new insights. Others are easily able to demonstrate the desired result of the strategy. Armed with this knowledge, you must adapt instruction to meet the needs of your students.

There are four categories of support you can provide for students who need scaffolding (Dickson, Collins, Simmons & Kame'enui, 1998):

- enlisting help for students from their peers, instructional aides, or other paraprofessionals

- manipulating the difficulty level of content that you are teaching (for example, providing an easier reading level that contains the same content)

- breaking down the content into smaller chunks to make it more manageable

- giving students organizers to clarify and guide their thinking through a task one step at a time

Within each technique described in this guide, there are examples of ways to scaffold and extend instruction to meet the needs of your students. *Scaffolding* provides support that targets cognitive complexity and student autonomy to reach rigor. *Extending* moves students who have already demonstrated the desired result to a higher level of understanding. These examples are provided as suggestions and should be adapted to target the specific needs of your students. Use them to spark ideas as you plan to meet the needs of your English language learners, students who receive special education or lack support at home, or simply the student who was absent the day before. The extension activities can help you plan for students in your gifted and talented program or those with a keen interest in the subject matter you are teaching.

Teacher Self-Reflection

You can use the questions below to self-reflect on your own level of confidence and competence with this strategy. Ideally, teachers will work collaboratively to implement examining similarities and differences and use the reflection questions to prompt discussions and sharing with colleagues. In addition, teachers can benefit from systematically gathering student reflections on their learning and perceptions of the instruction in the classroom. These multiple inputs can inform a teacher's self-reflection and plans for professional growth. Use the following set of reflection questions to guide you. The questions begin with reflecting on how to start the implementation process and move to progressively more complex ways of helping students examine similarities and differences.

- How can you begin to incorporate some aspect of this strategy in your instruction?

- What are some ways you can encourage your students to become more independent in their examination of similarities and differences?

- What are some ways you can check to see if most students are accurately identifying similarities and differences?

- What are ways you can adapt and create new techniques for identifying similarities and differences that address unique student needs and situations?

- What are you learning about your students as you adapt and create new techniques?

Instructional Techniques to Help Students Identify Similarities and Differences

There are many ways to help your students effectively interact with new knowledge and ultimately master the learning targets or standards of your grade level or content area. The ways you choose to design lessons that teach and show students how to identify similarities and differences will depend on your grade, the content, and the makeup of your class. These various ways or options are called instructional techniques. In the following sections of the book, you will find descriptions of how to implement these techniques for examining similarities and differences:

- Instructional Technique 1: Comparing using sentence stems, summarizers, and constructed responses

- Instructional Technique 2: Comparing using graphic organizers

- Instructional Technique 3: Classifying using sorting, matching, and categorizing

- Instructional Technique 4: Classifying using graphic organizers

- Instructional Technique 5: Comparing by Creating Metaphors and Similes

- Instructional Technique 6: Comparing by Creating Analogies

All of the techniques are similarly organized and include the following components:

- a brief introduction to the technique

- ways to effectively implement the technique

- common mistakes to avoid as you implement the technique

- examples and nonexamples from elementary and secondary classrooms using selected learning targets or standards from various documents

- ways to monitor for the desired result

- ways to scaffold and extend instruction to meet the needs of students

COMPARING USING SENTENCE STEMS, SUMMARIZERS, AND CONSTRUCTED RESPONSES

This technique provides three approaches to comparing two things: 1) sentence stems, 2) summarizing organizers, and 3) constructed responses. Sentence stems are most appropriate for younger students, students with limited experience writing in English, or students who are struggling with reading or the difficulty level of the content. The second approach uses a type of organizer known as a summarizer to notch up your expectations for students. Using this approach, students write a one-sentence summary describing the similarities and differences they identify in their comparison of two things. The third approach requires students to write a response to a prompt. A constructed response describes similarities (how aspects are alike) and differences (how aspects are different) in one or two paragraphs.

Ideally, you will become comfortable with all of these approaches so you can choose the one that best meets the needs of your students in a given instructional setting. Each approach is slightly more challenging than the previous one. Keep that in mind as you decide where to begin teaching your students how to make comparisons between two things.

Using Sentence Stems to Compare

Sentence stems appear at first glance to be a typical fill-in-the-blanks exercise. Indeed, students do fill in the blanks, but the blanks must be filled in with very specific information about the similarities and differences between two things. Table 1.1 contains a lesson plan for teaching your students how to use sentence stems for making comparisons using content text.

Table 1.1: A Lesson Plan for Making Comparisons Using Sentence Stems

Lesson Step	Description
1. Directly teach students the meanings of the following terms: *compare*, *similarities*, and *differences*.	As you give directions to students in the course of a lesson, or as they later encounter prompts on state assessments, they may be confused by unfamiliar terms. In other words, they may know how to do "it," but not recognize the way "it" is being described. If making comparisons using sentence stems is a technique that you will be using frequently, prepare a poster for students to consult when they are confused about what a term means. Use everyday examples to explain the terms. If you are accustomed to using the term *compare/contrast* to refer to comparison tasks, note that in the context of this guide, the term *compare* refers to its more traditional meaning of identifying similarities and dissimilarities between two things. However, if your students need to hear *compare/contrast* because that is the term used in your state standards and assessments, then make an adjustment to this lesson.
2. Directly teach students what a sentence stem is and the purpose of using it.	Explain that the sentence stems they will be using are designed to help them become experts at figuring out the similarities and differences between two things. Once again, use examples from familiar settings before expecting students to transfer their understandings of the terms and technique to content knowledge.
3. Create a sentence stem that requires students to compare two aspects of the content. Choose from one of the two sample stems.	You have several choices of sentence stem constructions to choose from: 1) a general comparison, 2) a more specific comparison, 3) an open-ended comparison, or 4) a comparison that requires a certain number of responses. Figure 1.1 contains examples of each of these types of sentence stems.
4. Choose content text that has what is generally referred to as a compare/contrast text structure. Then prepare a sentence stem that specifically correlates with the kind and number of comparisons in the text. After, model your reading of the text and the completion of the sentence stem for your students.	This modeling step is the most critical aspect of your lesson. Walk your students through the cognitive process, showing them how you make a comparison. Sentence stems are useful for simple comparisons of two things. Save more complicated comparisons for Instructional Technique 2, Comparing Using Graphic Organizers.

There are many varieties of sentence stems as noted in the lesson plan (Table 1.1) and Figure 1.1. As you start to implement this technique, you will likely provide students with the content-specific items you want them to compare. This assignment could come after students have listened to a brief lesson, read an article or section of content text, or watched a short video.

As students become more skilled at completing assigned sentence stems, transition them from using stems where you have chosen the items to be compared to expecting them to use stems in which they must identify the two things to be compared that were identified in the lesson, text, or video. This is part of releasing responsibility to students for listening, reading, and thinking on their own or with peers. Figure 1.1 contains partially completed stems as well as blank stems. Use the examples to guide your instruction. Resource A.1 contains a reproducible template of a sentence stem.

Figure 1.1: Examples of Sentence Stems

Type of Sentence Stem	Example
General stem comparing larger groups	Reptiles are like amphibians because _____ _____. Reptiles are different from amphibians because _____ _____.
Specific stem comparing two specific items	A frog and toad are alike because _____ and _____. They are different because _____, _____, and _____.
Open-ended stem that requires a certain number of responses	_____ and _____ are similar because they both _____. _____ and _____ are dissimilar because _____ is _____, but _____ is _____.

Using Summarizers to Compare

Summarizing is one way to ensure that students deepen their understanding of content knowledge in the process of making comparisons, thereby bringing closure to a comparing task. A summarizer is simply a graphic organizer that builds summarizing into the comparison process. The summarizer used in Figure 1.2 provides students with a planning and writing area in which to take notes in preparation for writing a one-sentence summary about their findings. Table 1.2 is a lesson plan for teaching students how to use this summarizer to compare two things. Figure 1.2 is an example of a completed summarizer. Many students and even some teachers find summarizing to be challenging, but with sufficient scaffolding and frequent opportunities to practice, summarizing can become a habit for your students. Use the following lesson to scaffold the summarizing process.

Table 1.2: A Lesson Plan for Teaching Students How to Use a Similarities and Differences Summarizer to Compare Two Things

Lesson Step	Discussion
1. Review the definitions you use in your classroom for the terms *summarizing, similarities,* and *differences.*	The definition of summarizing that you choose to use will depend on the maturity of your students. You may define a summary as a sentence in the students' own words describing the central idea and including some supporting details of a story or article. However, summarizing the results of examining similarities and differences requires that students engage in a somewhat deeper analysis of their findings, including explanations for why they have chosen to highlight certain similarities and differences.
2. Show students a blank summarizer—an organizer that provides a specific place on which students are to write their summaries. Explain to students that you will be modeling for them how to identify the similarities and differences between two cities using a blank copy of Figure 1.2.	You can adapt any graphic organizer you have designed for comparing one or more things to a summarizer by designating a specific space or area on the organizer in which a summary can be written.
3. Explain that once you have identified the similarities and differences between two things, you will write a summary in the summary box in the center column of the summarizer.	Remind students to pay close attention as you explain where you located the information you used to fill the summarizer (e.g., social studies book, Internet search, brochures from a travel agent). Also tell students to listen for your explanation about how you figured out the ways in which the cities were alike and different.
4. After you have filled in all of the boxes except the summary box, you have two choices: 1) if your students have been practicing writing summaries, challenge them to write a summary sentence using the information from the summarizer or 2) model writing the summary yourself.	As you model summarizing, show students how you experiment with various ideas and phrases found on the summarizer, writing down a phrase or two, reading it aloud to see if it makes sense, then crossing out words that don't sound right, and rewriting the sentence. Writing a good summary sentence may take several tries to get it just right.

Figure 1.2: Similarities and Differences Summarizer Comparing Two Cities in the United States

City #1 Tucson, Arizona	Summary Box Tucson, Arizona, a south-west desert community, and Honolulu, Hawaii, a tropical island paradise, are desirable, multicultural locations in which to live and vacation.	City #2 Honolulu, Hawaii
Differences	Similarities	Differences
Desert plants and animals	Cities in the United States	Tropical plants and animals
Mexican and Native American cultures	Favorite vacation spots for people all over the world	Japanese, Hawaiian, and Asian cultures
Landlocked	Multicultural	Surrounded by water
Gets little rain and has very low humidity	Residents and visitors can wear shorts and sandals most of the year	Tropical rain forest with very high humidity

Using a Constructed Response to Compare Two Things

A constructed response is a short answer that gives evidence of your students' mastery of a specific cognitive process (comparing), as applied to an aspect of content knowledge. In the context of this technique, students are asked to compare two things that are content specific and then generate a paragraph or two explaining the similarities and differences between the two things. Constructed responses often have a generic outline or template to guide students in their first attempts at constructing a response. One will be suggested for you as part of the sample lesson plan. The constructed response requires that students identify similarities and differences as well as organizing and writing the response. The constructed response also calls for students to make decisions about the relative importance of the identified similarities and differences. Table 1.3 displays a lesson plan for teaching your students how to write a short constructed response to answer a comparison question.

Table 1.3: Lesson Plan for Showing Students How to Generate a Constructed Response to Answer a Comparison Question

Lesson Step	Description
1. Select the two items, ideas, individuals, or concepts to be compared.	Choose the things to be compared from a specific area of content that is most important for students to understand. The goal of writing a constructed response is not to be able to write a constructed response. The goal in writing the response is to deepen students' knowledge of content. Do not waste processing opportunities on trivial or less-than-critical content.
2. Review the definitions for the terms *compare*, *constructed response*, *similarities*, and *differences*.	If you plan to have students write constructed responses regularly, create a poster containing the definitions and steps in this process.
3. There are two organizers to scaffold your students' writing of the constructed response. • Completed examples are found in Figures 1.3 and 1.4. • Display your own version of an empty planning and writing form on your screen or board on which you will list the attributes or categories being compared and the two things being compared.	Figure 1.3 lists the attributes or aspects of the items to be compared in the first column. The second and third columns contain the items to be compared: two cities in the United States. Note the question that is asked for each column: What is most important about the aspect?
4. Move through the categories one at a time, writing down the pertinent facts you have discovered in your research. After you have written down the facts, ask yourself the questions on the right.	• Are the two things being compared more different than alike? • Are the two things being compared more alike than different? • What is their most important similarity? • What is their most important difference?
5. Using the answers to the above questions, generate a topic sentence for your constructed response.	Write your topic sentence in the appropriate space in your organizer. Continue to evaluate each aspect from Figure 1.3 and write a sentence using supporting evidence from the figure.
6. Write these sentences on your constructed-response form, adding a conclusion.	See Figure 1.4 for a completed example.

Figure 1.3 An Organizer to Scaffold a Constructed Response Comparing Two Cities

Aspect of the city to be compared	City #1 Tucson, Arizona What is most important about the aspect?	City #2 Honolulu, Hawaii What is most important about the aspect?	Compare the two aspects
Location	United States Mainland	United States Hawaiian Islands	They are both states in the United States although Honolulu is on an island (Oahu) and Arizona is on the mainland.
Population	Population of 520,116 with a metropolitan-area population of 980,263	Population of 390,738 with a metropolitan-area population of 953,207	The cities are similar in the population sizes of their metropolitan areas although Honolulu is a smaller city in terms of population within actual city limits.
Cultures	Mexican American, Native American, and Caucasian	Asian, Hawaiian, and Caucasian	The cities are similar in that they both are home to a variety of cultures.
Climate	Hot and dry in the summer, moderate and warm in the winter	Warm and humid in some areas, but ocean breezes keep the weather moderate	The climates are similar in some ways (warmer temperatures).
Economy	Tourism and health care are major sources of economic strength.	Tourism, health care, and higher education are major sources of revenue in the city.	The cities are similar in that they depend on tourism for their economic strength as well as major hospitals, health care providers, and universities.

Prompt: After comparing the various aspects of two cities, take a position on whether they are more alike or more different and support that position with evidence from the "What is most important about the aspect?" boxes in Figure 1.3.

Figure 1.4 A Sample Comparison Constructed Response Comparing Two Cities

Organizational Structure	Planning Area
Topic sentence	Although Tucson and Honolulu have very different geographic locations, they are far more alike than different.
Location	Tucson is situated on the mainland in a landlocked area with hardly any natural bodies of water, while Honolulu is on an island surrounded by the Pacific Ocean. However, in all of the following aspects, the cities are very similar.
Population	Tucson and Honolulu are cities with about the same metropolitan population.
Cultures	They are both very multicultural with residents from varying backgrounds and homelands.
Climate	Even with its hot and dry summers, Tucson is similar to Honolulu in that it attracts many visitors from around the world to enjoy moderate temperatures and sunshine during the winter months.
Economy	Tourism, health care, and higher education are major contributors to the economies of both cities.
Conclusion sentence	Despite their different locations and geographic features, Tucson and Honolulu are both attractive cities in which to live, work, and vacation.

Common Mistakes

Most teachers have experienced the frustration of a lesson gone wrong. Learn from the mistakes of others before you plan your first lesson based on the various aspects of this technique. Here are some common mistakes to avoid when showing your students how to make comparisons using tools such as sentence stems, summarizers, and constructed responses:

- The teacher assumes that because key vocabulary has been introduced in prior lessons, students have mastered it.

- The teacher fails to review and remind students of key vocabulary meanings and usages.

- The teacher fails to take the time needed to directly teach and model the various processes for students.

- The teacher chooses content and text that is too difficult for students' first exposure to the various tools.

- The teacher does not release responsibility to students for doing the thinking necessary to complete sentence stems, summarizers, and constructed responses.

- The teacher provides answers and statements for students to copy into their sentence stems, summarizers, and writing and planning forms for constructed responses.

- The teacher fails to transition to more difficult tasks when students are ready for the challenge.

Examples and Nonexamples of Comparing Using Sentence Stems and Constructed Responses

The following examples and nonexamples demonstrate the use of various tools to make comparisons.

Elementary Example of Comparing Using Sentence Stems

The specific learning target being addressed in this example is *comparing and contrasting two or more versions of the same story* (CCSS English Language Arts Standard for Literacy RL.2.9). The class has listened to read-alouds and independently read the text of two versions of *Little Red Riding Hood*—one, the traditional tale, and the other, a Chinese version called *Lon Po Po.* Today, the teacher asks students to compare the two versions of the story. He gives each student a piece of paper with the following sentence stem written on the top half of the page: The story of Lon Po Po is like the story of Little Red Riding Hood because _____. The bottom half of the page contains this sentence stem: Lon Po Po is different from Little Red Riding Hood because _____. Here is how he introduces the activity.

> Today we are going to look for the things that are alike and different about two stories we have read: **Little Red Riding Hood** and **Lo Po Po**. Look at your think sheet. First, finish the sentence on the top half of the page by writing down the reason that the stories are alike. Then, finish the sentence stem on the bottom half of the page by writing down the reason that the stories are different.

The students come up with multiple similarities and differences, and the teacher asks them to share answers with their partners. He then hangs up two pieces of chart paper, writing *why the stories are alike* on one piece and *why the stories are different* on the other. Before a silent reading period begins, he directs each pair of partners to come up to the two pieces of chart paper, one pair at a time, and write down their similarities and differences. While the students are silently reading, the teacher has time to monitor their responses and note any students who have difficulties with similarities and differences. Following silent reading, the teacher holds a group discussion, asking students to point out the widespread agreement among the class members as well as some instances in which a student has identified a rather unusual similarity or difference. The teacher gives this student an opportunity to explain her thinking, therefore giving the class an opportunity to see how many different ways the text can be processed.

Elementary Nonexample of Sentence Stems

A second-grade teacher in a nearby classroom is working on the same learning target as the example teacher but has added a new wrinkle to the assignment. She asks her students to complete the following sentence stems after reading various fairy tales from other countries:

> *Cinderella, Princess Furball,* and *The Golden Sandal* are alike because _____.
>
> Fairy tales from other countries are different because
>
> _____.

She then asks students to complete the sentence stems in their reading journals and draw pictures of their favorite fairy tale character. The point of sentence stems is to guide students to compare two items and identify specific similarities and differences between those two items. This activity took both students and teacher off task.

Secondary Example of Comparing Using a Constructed Response

This secondary example uses two specific learning targets. The first learning target being addressed is *analyzing the debate over and reasons for United States entry into World War II* (Kansas Social Studies Curriculum Standards, 5.2.5). The second learning target is *analyzing how two or more texts address similar themes or topics in order to build knowledge or to compare the approaches the author takes* (CCR Anchor Standard 9 for Reading).

A high school teacher of American history wants his students to extend and deepen their knowledge regarding December 7, 1941, the attack on Pearl Harbor by Japan. He gives students two articles to read in advance of the lesson. The articles are written from different perspectives, and he wants his students to compare the approaches that the two authors take. He knows that comparing the articles from the author's point of view will not only give students a much deeper understanding of the content, but also enable them to become more skilled in their content reading and writing abilities. The teacher introduces the lesson in this way:

> Good morning, class. Today I'm privileged to have your English teacher here to team up with me. My area of expertise is history, and her expertise is English. We are working together to learn from each other and help you deepen your knowledge about a very significant event in the history of our country. You've read the textbook, and we've had some stimulating discussions about the bombing of Pearl Harbor, but our approach today is a bit different. Earlier in the week, I gave you two articles to read and discuss in your small groups. We are going to return to those articles and compare the approaches the two authors took to writing about Pearl Harbor.

The English teacher has prepared two templates similar to those found in Figures 1.3 and 1.4. Her template includes the following aspects of an author's approach: 1) What is the author's relationship to the topic? 2) How does the author organize thoughts and present information? 3) What is the author's attitude or posture toward the subject? and 4) What is the author's purpose for writing? The teachers decide to model the first question together. The English teacher explains to students some questions they can ask relative to the author's relationship to the topic, and the history teacher shares what he believes each author's perspective to be based on his content knowledge and knowledge about the authors. After modeling possible responses to the first question for both articles and writing them in the appropriate boxes on the organizer, the English teacher moves to the second aspect of an author's approach and explains some various possible ways authors can organize their thoughts. At this point, she asks students to work in their small groups to come up with a comparison between the two articles in terms of how the authors organized their thoughts and presented information. The teachers monitor how students are doing with identifying the similarities and differences between the two authors' approaches to the topic. With their background knowledge and previous reading of the articles prior to this lesson, the students are doing well. The teachers direct students to complete their organizers before class ends.

During the next class period, the teachers monitor students' progress on their organizers and help them begin writing their constructed responses comparing whether the articles are more alike or more different, supporting their positions with evidence from the text, and drafting their answers to the "what is most important about the aspect" question.

Secondary Nonexample of Using Constructed Responses to Identify Similarities and Differences

The nonexample history teacher uses the same learning targets as the example teacher. She believes that she will be able to show her students how to compare the approaches two authors took to writing about the same historical event. In fact, she chooses the same articles as the example teacher, reads them carefully, and completes both organizers. She then hands out blank organizers to her students and proceeds to go through each aspect line by line asking students to copy her notes from the board. The teacher has done all of the thinking work and shortchanged her students' learning as a result. Furthermore, she and her students have missed out on a rich interdisciplinary experience that held promise for deepening content knowledge as well as developing reading and writing skills in a specific discipline.

Determining If Students Can Make a Comparison between Two Things

The only way to determine if your direct teaching and modeling to show students how to identify similarities and differences is successful is to have students explain, write, or otherwise represent the critical content for you.

Here is a list of ways you can monitor whether your students are able to identify critical content as a result of their making comparisons:

- Students can explain how examining similarities and differences has deepened their understanding of content.

- Students can support their explanation of similarities and differences with evidence from the text.

- Students are able to create their own sentence stems to explain the similarities and differences they find in various forms of content.

- Students can summarize what they have learned from a lesson or text.

- Students can develop a constructed response that summarizes the important similarities and differences between two things.

The student proficiency scale for making comparisons between two things (see Table 1.4) will help you assess how well your students are progressing in identifying similarities and differences related to critical content. Use this scale to help you monitor for the desired result of making comparisons between two concepts, ideas, or other items.

Table 1.4: Student Proficiency Scale for Comparing Using Sentence Stems, Summarizers, and Constructed Responses

Emerging	Fundamental	Desired Result
Students are able to make basic comparisons between topics. Students can state what the comparison was about.	Students are able to make comparisons between topics. Students are able to explain comparisons that are already made.	Students can make multiple comparisons between topics that demonstrate knowledge of the critical content. Students summarize the critical content as it relates to the comparison they drew. Students are able to summarize what they learned as a result of comparing.

Scaffold and Extend Instruction to Meet Students' Needs

The ways in which you scaffold or extend making comparisons between two things will depend on which of the three approaches you choose to use with your students.

Scaffolding

- For students experiencing difficulties with sentence stems, go back one step and list a few characteristics of each item to be compared in a side-by-side fashion to help students make the comparisons more readily.

- For students experiencing difficulties with summarizing, provide students with sentence stems or graphic organizers to help them organize their thoughts.

- Choose content or text that is slightly easier to teach a technique.

- Pair students with stronger peers to provide role models.

- Accept sets of words and phrases or short answers to questions as an intermediate step in writing constructed responses.

Extending

- Provide sentence stems that are more open ended or that put together more complex concepts to be compared.

- Assign some students the task of creating their own sentence stems, using comparing, classifying, or analogies.

- Have some students gather all responses from the class and generalize the similarities and differences for that task and ask them to model their thinking for the class.

COMPARING USING GRAPHIC ORGANIZERS

As your students become more skilled at making comparisons between two things, concepts, or ideas, notch up your expectations by introducing them to a set of organizers that are specifically intended for making comparisons between two or more items: 1) Venn diagram, 2) double-bubble diagram, 3) comparison matrix, and 4) modified T-chart. Reproducible templates of these organizers can be found in Resources A.2 through A.5.

There are two instructional approaches to help your students become skilled at examining similarities and differences using graphic organizers. The first approach is teacher directed in which you select the ideas, events, or things to be compared and explicitly tell students the important attributes or criteria you want them to use for comparison. This teacher-directed method ensures that students spend their time considering the most important content characteristics and guarantees that almost all students will respond with conclusions that are reasonably correct. This structured approach is a good way to begin, especially when you want all students to learn specific critical information.

Another way to approach comparison activities is more student managed. Using this approach, you may or may not identify the items to be compared but will generally give students the responsibility for determining key attributes to use for comparison. You might even ask students to select the items being compared. Because this activity is more open ended, students are likely to come up with different answers and different conclusions from each other, making for more interesting group discussions and more diverse findings. Become comfortable with releasing responsibility to students for doing the thinking required for making comparisons using graphic organizers.

How to Effectively Implement Comparing Using Graphic Organizers

Learning to make comparisons using graphic organizers requires teaching your students how to almost simultaneously execute two different sets of skills: 1) making comparisons and 2) translating the information derived from making those comparisons to a specific graphic organizer.

There are four mental substeps involved in the overall cognitive process of making comparisons: 1) choosing exactly what will be compared—for example, words, numbers, ideas, events, concepts, persons, places, or things; 2) identifying the critical attributes or the most important characteristics of each of the items to be compared; 3) determining whether the attributes or characteristics are alike or different; and 4) summarizing or drawing conclusions (generalizing) about the overall findings.

The most challenging step of the four for learners who lack background knowledge about content will likely be Step 2: identifying the critical attributes of the various items to be compared. Figure 2.1 leads you and your students through the steps of identifying the critical attribute of just one thing. In order to compare, you will need to engage in this exercise for at least two and possibly more things, depending on your content and the organizer you select.

At the same time that learners are making comparisons about critical content, they must also be applying what they know about how the various organizers described in this technique work. Students need to know which of the similarities and differences they are generating from their comparison are important enough to be recorded and precisely where this information should be recorded on a given organizer. The more involved your students can be in every step, the more content knowledge they will take away from the experience. However, effectively implementing comparing using the more sophisticated graphic organizers in this technique must be a gradual process for you and possibly many of your students.

There are four graphic organizers that are uniquely suited to comparing two or more things: 1) Venn diagram, 2) double-bubble diagram, 3) comparison matrix, and 4) modified T-chart. You will find completed examples with classroom content illustrating each organizer in this section.

Figure 2.1: Steps to Identifying the Critical Attributes of One Thing

Step	Example
1. Choose an important person, place, thing, or event from content being studied as your subject for identifying critical attributes.	List the attributes of the famous brass fanfare section of the musical composition "The William Tell Overture" by Rossini.
2. Break down the subject into its component parts or attributes and list them. These are called "nondefining" attributes.	Loud Fast Bright Staccato
3. Generalize categories for each specific attribute. Give the category a name. These are called "defining" attributes.	Dynamics Tempo Timbre Articulation
4. Use this list of attributes as a starting point for a comparison activity.	Compare the ending brass fanfare section of "The William Tell Overture" to the opening lyrical string introduction in the same composition. Use the categories (defining attributes) of dynamics, tempo, timbre, and articulation to describe the second passage. Summarize similarities and differences between the two.

Venn Diagram

A Venn diagram consists of two or more overlapping circles that can be used for specific, general, abstract, or concrete comparison activities. Figure 2.2 shows the versatility of the Venn diagram.

Figure 2.2: When to Use a Venn Diagram

Purpose	When to Use a Venn Diagram	Examples
Specific	When it's important for students to know specific facts or important examples	Factors of 18 and 24
General	When students need to be able to compare generalized ideas drawn from specifics	Healthy eating habits and weight loss techniques
Abstract	When students are ready to compare and contrast abstract ideas they have gleaned through deeper learning	Literary themes of different authors
Concrete	When manipulating physical objects is feasible, appropriate, and helpful to students	Sorting shapes according to different attributes

Each circle of a Venn diagram is labeled with one of the items being compared. The differences are written or drawn in the outer circles and the similarities are put into the area of intersection, showing that those items belong to both or all circles. Figure 2.3 displays a comparison of the factors of 18 and 24.

Figure 2.3: Venn Diagram Comparing Factors of 18 and 24

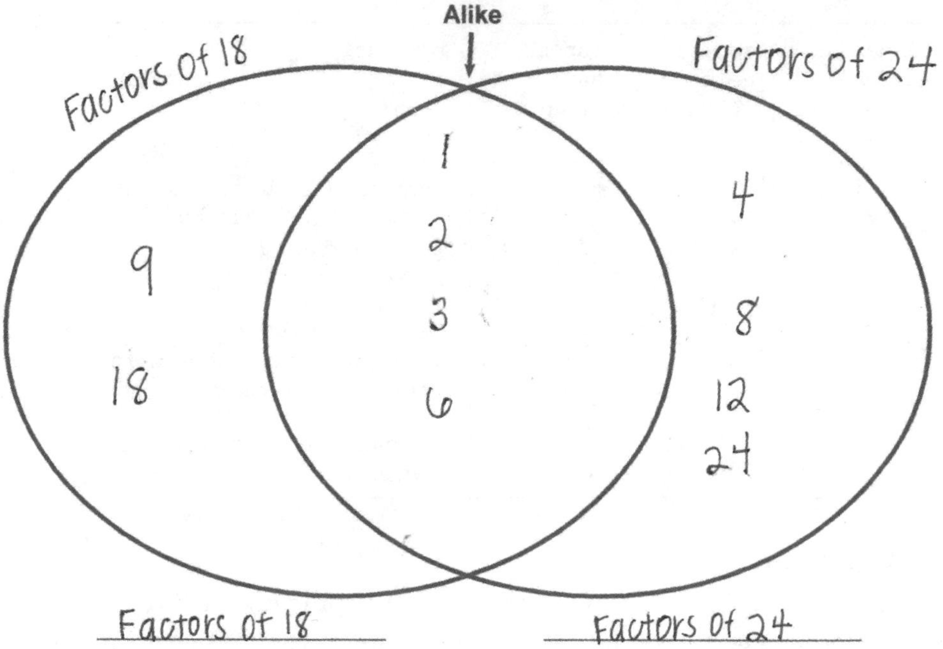

What I notice about the similarities and differences:

Common Factors of 18 and 24 are 1,2,3, and 6

6 is the Greatest Common Factor.

To add complexity to the task, add another circle to create a triple Venn diagram. To construct this diagram, students must determine which items are members of one, two, or all three circle sets. Figure 2.4 displays a triple comparison of the factors of 18, 21, and 24.

Figure 2.4: Triple Venn Diagram Comparing Factors of 18, 21, and 24

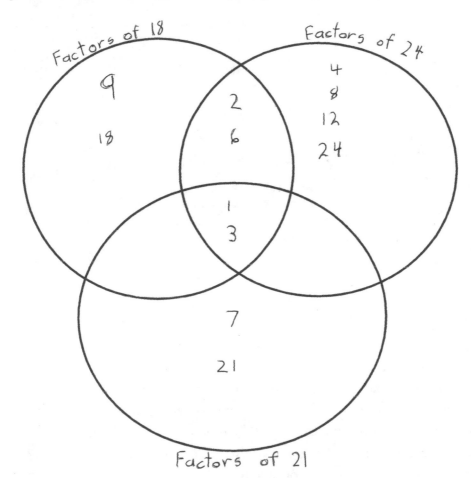

Double-Bubble Diagrams

The double-bubble diagram (Hyerle, 1996) is a variation of the Venn diagram and is recommended for use with students who may need scaffolding before transitioning to a traditional Venn. Items being compared are written or drawn in the two shaded circles known as *anchor bubbles*. The distinguishing characteristics (critical attributes) of each topic are written to the sides of each anchor bubble, one item per bubble. Students can add bubbles if they have more ideas. The features in common are written in the middle bubbles— one similar attribute per bubble. Color coding the bubbles can aid students further. Figure 2.5 illustrates a double-bubble diagram comparing stringed instruments.

Figure 2.5: Double-Bubble Diagram Comparing Stringed Instruments

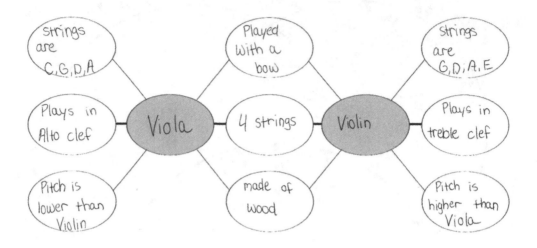

Adapted from Hyerle (1996).

Comparison Matrix

A comparison matrix is a third type of graphic organizer for comparing two or more people, things, events, or concepts in terms of certain characteristics. The comparison matrix is a grid with the names of things being compared written across the top—one per column—and the characteristics written along the side, one at the start of each row. Students record data in each cell of the grid. The final column can be used to generalize the similarities and differences among the concepts in that row. A three-by-two or a three-by-three matrix is a reasonable task to have students complete. However, take care not to make this task too complex by comparing too many things or having too many criteria. Figure 2.6 displays a completed example of a comparison matrix for cultures in a state.

Figure 2.6: Comparison Matrix of Cultures in a State

	Amish	Appalachian	Latino	Important Similarities and Differences
Traditions and Beliefs	Simple, plain life Teach children their way of life No modern things like electricity, cars Strong belief in God and hard work	Love of nature Strong belief in God Handmade things Storytelling Independent and happy to live where they do Help each other but don't like change in their land	Roman Catholic Keep the Spanish language at home Fiestas Work is important	**Same:** Strong belief in God Teach their beliefs to children **Different:** Type of religion
Family	Family is center of daily life Father is head of family, women are respected	Strong ties Loyalty to family Women are important and sometimes act as head of family	Close knit Includes relatives Respect for older people Help others in family in need	**Same:** Strong family ties **Different:** Head of family

Modified T-Chart

The fourth and final graphic organizer described in this technique is a modified T-chart that can be used to compare two or more things. It includes the same information as a Venn diagram, with the addition of a dedicated space in which students can write new insights gained from their analyses of similarities and differences. There are spaces for both likenesses and differences. Defined attributes may be listed inside the arrows connecting the two boxes. This chart gives you some flexibility in how much structure to provide your students. You can complete parts of this organizer ahead of time and assign students to do the rest, or leave it open ended and have students select the items to be compared as well as attributes to be used. An example of a completed organizer comparing the Greek and Roman empires is displayed in Figure 2.7.

Figure 2.7: Modified T-Chart Comparing the Greek and Roman Empires

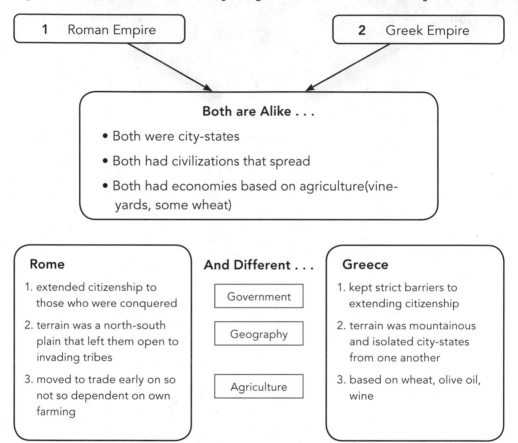

And So, in Summary . . .

Common Mistakes

There are many ways teachers can confuse students when combining instruction for comparing two or more things while also becoming skilled in choosing and using specific organizers for examining similarities and differences:

- The teacher fails to choose an appropriate organizer for the critical content to be mastered.

- The teacher fails to provide enough direct teaching and modeling of the content, leaving students with only a partial version of the critical content.

- The teacher fails to provide enough direct teaching and modeling of how to execute various organizers.

- The teacher talks too much and fails to allow students opportunities for processing with classmates.

- The teacher fails to include the final step of either generalizing or summarizing their findings about similarities and differences.

- The teacher fails to place enough emphasis on important aspects of the content, thereby depriving students of opportunities to deepen their content knowledge.

Examples of Comparing Using Graphic Organizers in the Classroom

Identifying similarities and differences using organizers requires solid content knowledge and advance planning. Following are examples and non-examples from elementary and secondary classrooms.

Elementary Example of Comparing Using Graphic Organizers

This elementary example illustrates a teacher using a comparison matrix (shown earlier in Figure 2.6) in a third-grade social studies class. The specific learning target being addressed is *describing similarities and differences between cultural groups and activities in Ohio and during the past and present* (Ohio Social Studies Standards: HIS.3.4a). The students have read various resource books and watched videos to learn critical content about the Amish, Latino, and Appalachian cultures. In the course of their introduction to this new knowledge, students identify two common attribute categories present in each culture: 1) traditions and 2) beliefs and family. Here is how the teacher introduced the matrix to her students:

> Class, we've been learning many facts about three different cultural groups that live in our state. Today we are going to organize some of the facts we have been learning into a graphic organizer called a comparison matrix. *The teacher reviews the meaning of the term* comparing *for students and explains that a matrix is an arrangement of things that are connected. She displays a copy of the blank matrix containing the labels.* You are going to compare two kinds of facts (facts about traditions and beliefs and facts about the structure of their families) for three different cultural groups (Amish, Latino, and Appalachian). Remember we are comparing, so your job is to look for facts about the three groups that are either similar or different.

The teacher passes out a copy of the organizer to each group and walks around the classroom visiting them to monitor the accuracy of the students' information. Once the groups complete their organizers, she asks them to come up with some concluding statements about each criterion.

Elementary Nonexample of Comparing Using Graphic Organizers

In the nonexample elementary classroom, the teacher is teaching to the same standard. He decides to have his students compare the same three cultures—Amish, Appalachian, and Latino—but thinks it is important for students to consider as many different aspects as possible about all of the cultures. He gives them a matrix with three columns and six rows, one each for traditions and beliefs, family, food, art and music, and language. He soon realizes that the assignment is too complex for his students. He later takes his lesson back to the drawing board to scale it down so that his students can process the content more readily.

Comparing Using Graphic Organizers in the Secondary Classroom

The secondary example/nonexample is based on the following specific learning target: *learning how large-scale empires arose in the Mediterranean basin between 500 BCE and 300 CE* (National Center for History in the Schools: History Standards: World History Era 3: Standard #3).

Secondary Example of Comparing Using Graphic Organizers

A middle school teacher chooses a modified T-chart graphic organizer to help his students gain deeper knowledge about the learning target. Most of the class has mastered the foundational knowledge of the unit and is ready to expand this knowledge. The teacher introduces the lesson this way:

> Class, you have done excellent work during our studies of the Greek and Roman empires. Today we are going to think about these two empires in a comparative way, to figure out how these empires are alike and how they are different. Your first task is to choose the characteristics you will use to compare the two empires.

For some students who need scaffolding, the teacher chooses the criteria. Students work in pairs to complete the task. Because the modified T-chart includes a summary section, the teacher immediately knows if his students achieve the desired effect of using the organizer. Figure 2.7, shown earlier following the description of a modified T-chart, is an example of the work of one group of students.

Secondary Nonexample of Graphic Organizers

The nonexample teacher also teaches middle school students, and her learning target is identical to the one selected by the example teacher. However, she decides to use a Venn diagram and fails to provide her students with instruction and modeling about how to complete the assignment. Her students write their similarities and differences in random places on the diagram, and she quickly realizes that she has failed to give students a sufficient model or explanation in advance. She has made some faulty assumptions about the skills of her students and was further tripped up by choosing an organizer that was ill suited for the task.

Determining If Students Can Compare Using Graphic Organizers

Take time to monitor whether the majority of students are accurately recording similarities and differences as they use graphic organizers. If students are given the task of identifying criteria by which to compare the topics, make sure they have selected important criteria so that they will gain a deeper understanding of which content is most important. Here are some ways effective teachers monitor their students' understanding:

- Have students work in pairs or small groups to complete their graphic organizers. Closely monitor students' efforts, checking responses and information recorded, prompting and guiding with questions to encourage rigor.

- Explain how the organizer represents their understanding of the similarities and differences in content.

- Write summary statements about what is most important to remember about the similarities and differences in various aspects of content.

- After students have examined similarities and differences using graphic organizers, have them switch papers. Pose questions to the whole class, allowing students to locate the answers on their peers' papers.

- Give students different graphic organizers to choose from once they have had opportunities to practice different types.

Table 2.1 contains a student proficiency scale for making comparisons between two or more things using graphic organizers. Use and adapt as needed to determine how your students are progressing from taking their first steps to the desired result.

Table 2.1: Student Proficiency Scale for Making Comparisons Using Graphic Organizers

Emerging	Fundamental	Desired Result
Students are able to compare some concepts using a simple graphic organizer. Students can state what the comparison is about.	Students accurately use a graphic organizer to compare content concepts. Students can choose appropriately which graphic organizer to use. Students can state which critical content they are comparing.	Students are able to choose or create a graphic organizer to make comparisons. Students accurately use a graphic organizer to show how two topics compare. Students can explain how the organizer helps them better understand the critical content. Students initiate the use of organizers on their own.

Scaffold and Extend Instruction to Meet Students' Needs

As you become more skilled at choosing and using graphic organizers to help students deeply understand similarities and differences of critical content topics, you will more readily identify students who need adaptations from your original instruction. Some students need support or scaffolding, while others are ready to be challenged through extensions. Following are some suggestions that might help you zero in on the precise needs of your students.

Scaffolding

- Provide students with critical prerequisites in an organizer so they can realize progress in completing the organizer.

- Provide the elements and attributes that students should use in their comparison matrices and provide a review of each element or attribute.

- Use the attribute chart shown in Figure 2.1 to give students frequent practice in listing the critical attributes of various content-related topics.

Extending

- Release responsibility to students for selecting the elements and attributes of their content-related comparisons.

- Encourage students to construct a triple Venn diagram to make the task more complex.

- Give students more unusual comparisons to make within the content.

CLASSIFYING USING SORTING, MATCHING, AND CATEGORIZING

Classifying is the second major cognitive process that helps students identify similarities and differences in critical content. Classifying is the grouping of things that are alike into categories based on their attributes, characteristics, features, or properties. There are three discrete classifying activities: 1) sorting, 2) matching, and 3) categorizing. Figure 3.1 describes precisely what your students will be doing when they sort, match, or categorize. Classifying, whether sorting, matching, or categorizing, demands a precise and specific kind of discrimination to identify often minute similarities or differences that can easily be overlooked.

Classifying may at first glance appear to be simple because many basic early childhood tasks involve one or more of these subprocesses. However, it can become extremely challenging as the content increases in difficulty. To sort, match, and categorize, students need both deep and wide content knowledge. The more background knowledge students have, the more readily they can classify successfully.

Figure 3.1: Three Types of Classifying

Type of Classifying	Student Outcome
Sorting	When presented with specific categories by the teacher, students can sort content into these categories based on their similar attributes.
Matching	When presented with various types of content, students can match two or more things based either on their sameness or equivalence. This equivalence could exist in the form of a definition and picture that go together; a picture and description that match; various mathematical expressions that, when solved, express identical values; or the matching of uppercase and lowercase letters that express different forms of the same alphabet letter.
Categorizing	When presented with a list of elements, students can organize them into two or more categories, explain the critical attributes of the categories they have selected, and explain and defend why each element belongs in a specific category.

How to Effectively Implement Classifying Using Sorting, Matching, and Categorizing

The effective implementation of classifying requires that you directly teach and model for students how to identify similarities and differences in various things and then to group those things based on their similarities and differences.

Using Sorting to Identify Similarities and Differences

Activities designed for analyzing and categorizing words, numbers, shapes, or other manipulatives according to their characteristics are often called sorts. The purpose of sorting is to help students focus on a conceptual or structural feature of an object or idea. With words, that means looking closely at meanings, sounds, spelling patterns, or usage. With numbers, students consider properties, values, divisibility, resulting graphs, and so on. Shapes can be sorted. So can rocks or sports equipment, and so can just about any type of artifact related to content you are teaching. Sorting implies a hands-on activity, so having objects or cards with words or pictures printed on them works best. To design a sorting activity, follow these steps:

- Choose a content-area skill or concept and decide whether it will be a closed sort or open sort. A closed sort is one for which you select the categories that your students will place things in. An open sort is when students create their own categories based on groupings they have created. This kind of sort is called categorizing and is best suited to older students with deeper content knowledge.

- Gather six to twenty objects or cards labeled with pictures, words, or numbers. Each group of students will need the same collection of things to sort.

- For a closed sort, include a mat labeled with category headings or category cards to put at the top of a group. Have students explain their process of sorting or their reasoning for grouping certain things together. Summarize after everything has been sorted by asking students to generalize about the similarities and differences they discovered in this activity.

Using Matching to Identify Similarities and Differences

Matching activities require students to find things that are the same or equivalent. In the simplest example of matching, preschool children search for a triangle shape from a larger collection of shapes to place next to the drawing of a triangle on their worksheets. Each shape they choose from the jumble of shapes in their collection must be carefully examined to discriminate between the shape on the paper and the shape in their hands.

Matching activities can also focus on equivalence rather than sameness. Another simple example is matching upper- and lowercase letter manipulatives. This calls for a greater depth of knowledge and may require scaffolding in the form of a chart where students can consult the twenty-six matched pairs of upper- and lowercase letters to scaffold their sorting.

There are more sophisticated ways to have your students identify similarities and differences through equivalence matching—for example, using pictures and definitions of planets, types of rocks, or other categories of science content. This type of matching calls for students to pay close attention to the descriptions in the definitions to match the details of the objects in the photos. Matching equivalent expressions in mathematics is another way to hold students accountable for noticing the specific details of content.

To design a matching activity, follow these steps:

- Choose an aspect of content that requires students to pay close attention to details or structural features.

- Identify the attributes or characteristics to be analyzed—for example, the colors, shapes, and configurations in certain types of rock formations.

- Model for students how these attributes and characteristics are alike and different.

- Explain further that the similarities and differences between these attributes and characteristics must be described precisely to determine equivalence between the photo and description. There can be no discrepancies if there is to be a match.

Using Categorization to Identify Similarities

Categorization is the third of the three ways to classify things. As noted earlier, categorization requires a greater depth of knowledge about a specific content area. Students are expected to consider a greater number of items or concepts and determine how best to categorize them into two or more categories. To design a categorizing activity, use the following steps:

- Give students a list of concepts, ideas, places, people, or things. In the beginning stage of implementing categorization activities, encourage students to cut their written lists into strips so they can physically place them in different categories.

- Ask students to identify the important attributes of each item on their lists to see if they can discover some common attributes to help them categorize.

- Once they have identified the categories, ask students to move their strips around between the categories. Categorizing takes time and thinking. More substantive categorizing exercises benefit from students taking a break and coming back later to see whether the previous categorization immediately makes sense or feels wrong.

- If students have been moving strips of paper around, direct them to make a final choice of location and then create a permanent record of their groupings.

- Ask students to explain and defend their selection of categories and assignment of items to those categories.

- Discuss with students whether the categories they have selected are superordinate categories containing many items (e.g., vehicles) or subordinate categories that may also be further subdivided (e.g., automobiles, RVs, SUVs, pickup trucks, vans, semis). Ask students to explain the relationships between the items on their list and their categories.

Common Mistakes

Here are some common mistakes that teachers can make while implementing classifying using sorting, matching, and categorizing:

- The teacher does not directly teach or model classifying for students.

- The teacher accepts incorrect classification of content.

- The teacher asks students to classify information they have not been introduced to or learned.

- The teacher asks students to classify information that is trivial or unrelated to critical content.

Examples and Nonexamples of Classification

Although the grade levels and learning targets may differ from your own experience, view the following examples and nonexamples as a way to more effectively implement classification of critical content in your classroom.

Elementary Example of Classification Using Sorting

The specific learning target being addressed is *plan and conduct an investigation to describe and classify different kinds of materials by their observable properties* (Next Generation Science Standards 2-PS1-1). The second-grade teacher gathers a number of similar objects made of different materials: plastic and wooden rulers; plastic and glass soda bottles; and wooden, metal, and plastic spoons. The goal of the lesson is to have students identify observable properties of various objects to better describe and sort them. The properties the students will consider are size, shape, hardness, and sinks/floats. The teacher plans that this activity will go on throughout the week as each group of four students goes to the counter during various open time slots during the day and fills out a properties chart. Earlier in the day, the teacher placed her materials on a long counter that stretches the length of her classroom.

> Boys and girls, I know you are very curious about all of the objects I put on the counter. Today we are going to investigate the properties of these various objects and sort them into different categories according to those properties. Properties are characteristics of objects. *The teacher writes the list of properties up on the board: size, shape, hardness, and sinks/floats.* Let's read through the list together.

The teacher gives each pod of four students a blank copy of the sorting chart shown in its completed version in Figure 3.2. She assigns roles for each student in a group: Recorder, Observers 1 and 2, and Manipulator (the student who will place the objects in the water). She then explains the attributes of each of the categories and asks the students how they can classify the objects in the categories. Students discuss in their groups how they can see size and shape but need to put the object in water to see if it floats or sinks. The teacher walks around and guides groups to think through how to test properties before they start the investigation.

Once all students have manipulated the objects and each group has completed its properties chart, the teacher leads a discussion about conclusions the students have made. They agree after much discussion and replication that objects that are hard, heavy, and solid sink in the water. Objects that float are more lightweight and flexible. Wood is lighter than metal. Plastic is lighter than glass. The students have been able to examine similarities and differences in critical content, deepen their knowledge, and will continue to build knowledge as they do experiments at home with various objects.

Figure 3.2: Sorting Objects According to Their Properties

Object	Size			Hardness			Weight		What It Does in Water	
	Small	Medium	Large	Soft-Squishy	Hard-Firm	Flexible-Bendy	Light	Heavy	Sinks	Floats
Plastic Ruler		X				X	X			X
Wooden Ruler		X			X		X			
Plastic Soda Bottle		X		X				X		X
Glass Soda Bottle			X		X			X	X	
Wooden Spoon			X		X		X			X
Plastic Spoon	X					X	X			X
Metal Teaspoon	X				X		X		X	

Elementary Nonexample of Classification Using Sorting

The nonexample teacher is using the same learning target. She decides to challenge her students by presenting them with the objects and letting them come up with a list of possible physical attributes that describe the items. Each pod of four desks has a full set of all of the objects so students can readily handle and examine them. However, in the absence of clear categories and the teacher modeling exactly what students need to do, the students play with the objects rather than develop a list of physical properties. She assumed that her students would be able to skip important aspects of the lesson such as directly teaching and modeling.

Secondary Example of Classification Using Categorization

The specific learning target being addressed is *using references to compare the physical properties of the planets* (Utah Sixth Grade Science Core Curriculum, UT.6.III.1.b). The sixth-grade science teacher has been working with students on understanding the relationships and attributes of objects in the solar system. Students have some basic knowledge, but the teacher wants them to use some appropriate digital resources as well as their textbook and other resource materials to classify the planets in each of four different categories: size, composition, distance from the sun, and historical information.

> Class, today we're going to classify the planets in four different ways. I'm going to model for you how I would classify the planets by size. I have some ideas already from reading the textbook and consulting the many resources the media specialist found for us. But, I also want to check the Internet to see if there's anything there that might help me figure out how many categories I might need to classify planets by size.

The teacher models the research process, accessing three different websites that have information about planets. She tells students as she begins her search that she does not have a firm idea of the categories she will use for describing the relative sizes of the planets. She models for students how she chooses the three categories seen in Figure 3.3. She explains to students that they will decide how to classify the planets by composition. She hands out a blank organizer and works with students to fill in the titles of each column: Composition Categories, Planet(s) in This Category, and Descriptive Information. Students work in small groups while the teacher spends time with each group monitoring the students' discussion and seeing what they are writing on their organizers. Each group takes a turn at accessing the classroom online computer. Once students have completed their organizers, they make some generalizations about their findings. The majority of students were able to complete their organizers. Later they will have opportunities to work on at least one more. The teacher is pleased that their knowledge of the solar system is becoming more nuanced, and they are discovering that in many cases that knowledge about the solar system is still changing.

Figure 3.3: Classifying Planets Using Categorization

Size Categories	Planet(s) in This Category	Descriptive Information
Small Planets	Mercury, Venus, Earth, and Mars	Diameters less than 8,000 miles.
Lesser Planets	Mercury and Pluto	As of 2006, Pluto is no longer considered to be a planet. It's called a dwarf planet. Mercury is the smallest planet.
Giant Planets	Jupiter, Saturn, Uranus, and Neptune	Diameters greater than 30,000 miles. Sometimes called the gas giants.

Nonexample of Secondary Classification Using Categorization

The nonexample teacher is working toward the same specific learning target. He has a far more ambitious agenda for his students than the example teacher. He divides his class into small groups of six students and assigns each group one of the four attributes: size, composition, distance from the sun, and historical information. He doesn't take the time to model the process and expects each group to come up with its own categories in which to place the planets. Some groups had a student or two who could figure things out, but too many students were confused. The teacher's biggest mistake was failing to model and directly teach the process.

Determining If Students Can Identify Similarities and Differences in Critical Content Using Classifying

To determine if your students have achieved the desired result of this technique, two conditions need to be in place:

1. Your students need to engage in an action or produce a product to demonstrate their knowledge of the critical content.

2. You, the teacher, must engage in some kind of monitoring action (listen, look for, read, check, inspect, etc.) to determine if your students can indeed classify critical content in meaningful ways and explain the underlying reasons for their thinking.

Here are some ways to monitor your students' progress toward the desired result of classifying using sorting, matching, or categorizing:

- Students are able to work with partners to sort, match, and categorize appropriately.

- Students are able to generate their own classification categories.

- Students can orally explain or summarize in writing the reasons they have chosen certain categories and how the activity has expanded their knowledge of critical content.

- Students can complete a classifying chart using information obtained from classroom resources.

- Students confer with peers and revise their categories and/or classifications in their organizers while the teacher walks around the classroom and attends to conversations.

- Students generate a list of attributes associated with each category on their comparison charts and turn them in for the teacher to check.

- Students summarize what they learned from classifying content either orally or in writing.

Use the scale in Table 3.1 to determine the progression of your students' abilities.

Table 3.1: Student Proficiency Scale for Classifying Using Sorting, Matching, and Categorizing

Emerging	Fundamental	Desired Result
Students can explain a classification that was done by someone else. Students can determine some characteristics of the critical content related to classifying. Students can explain what they are classifying.	Students can determine appropriate categories using critical characteristics. Students summarize the results of their classification.	Students are able to explain the decisions they make while they classify. Students are able to explain how the classification relates to critical content.

Scaffold and Extend Instruction to Meet Students' Needs

When you have students in your classroom who find classifying critical content to be difficult, along with students at the opposite end of the learning continuum who have already mastered the skills you are teaching, you need to adapt by scaffolding or extending instruction to meet these diverse needs.

Scaffolding

- Provide students with predetermined categories for sorting activities.

- Present simple examples using more familiar knowledge before expecting students to classify critical content.

- Provide more explicit modeling and thinking aloud about the classifying processes.

- Provide instructions one at a time to give students opportunities to execute a task before moving on to the next one.

- Use fewer categories and fewer items to sort, match, or categorize.

Extending

- Ask students to develop their own organizers for classifying content knowledge.

- Expect students to provide more written summaries and constructed responses about the results of their classification activities.

- Ask students to classify critical content by adding more detailed categories and subcategories.

Instructional Technique 4

CLASSIFYING USING GRAPHIC ORGANIZERS

Classifying is the process of grouping things that are alike into categories based on their characteristics. When classifying, you and your students will concentrate on finding things that are alike. In instances where the items to be classified are more complex than the types of sorting, matching, and categorizing we did in the previous technique, graphic organizers give students ways to practice and deepen their understanding of the content in more analytical ways. Figure 4.1 explains the steps that you and your students will use when classifying critical content. Column 1 lists the individual steps in classifying, while Column 2 describes a simple example of the step.

Figure 4.1: Steps for Classifying Critical Content

Step	Example
Select the set of items that need to be classified.	The set of items to be classified comprises all of the vocabulary words listed on the board for today's story.
Determine the major superordinate categories represented in the set of items.	The list of words can be classified in several different ways. It contains verbs, nouns, adjectives, and conjunctions.
Name the superordinate category to which the concept belongs and explain why it belongs in that category.	All of these categories belong to the superordinate category known as parts of speech.
Identify any subordinate categories for the concept and explain why they belong in the category.	The list of nouns has the following subordinate categories: persons, places, or things. The nouns in the list include *Little Red Riding Hood, Grandmother, basket, forest,* and *cape.* The items on this list are either persons, places, or things, so they belong in the noun category.

How to Effectively Implement Classifying Using Graphic Organizers

Three graphic organizers are specifically intended for classifying tasks: 1) classification charts, 2) affinity diagrams, and 3) dichotomous flowcharts and keys. Once you become familiar with these organizers, you will find multiple ways to classify information for any and all of the content areas you teach.

Classification Charts

A classification chart is one way for students to classify things using a structured chart or grid to record groupings listed under a category heading. To do this activity, provide students with a grid that has categories written as headings for each column as shown in Figure 4.2. In addition, provide students with a list of elements to classify. Students should find a column for each element on the list. This is the simplest and most teacher-directed way to use this activity. For more student-led use of classification charts, you can provide very open-ended assignments such as asking students to classify the science vocabulary list for the week or classify the chemicals on the periodic table.

Figure 4.2: Classification Chart for Verb Tenses

Present Tense Verbs	Past Tense Verbs	Future Tense Verbs

To increase student engagement, transform this activity into an academic game of Categories, similar to the popular game Scattergories, as shown in Figure 4.3. Add a column to the left of the chart and have students write any word, one letter per row. They can use their first names. They have to complete the chart, but this time using an example that starts with the letter at the head of the row.

After students complete the chart, have them explain what they noticed and identify similarities among elements in each column and differences from column to column. Students should be able to articulate similarities and differences in the content after completing this activity.

Figure 4.3: Categories Game Classification Chart for French Verbs

	Present Tense Verbs	Past Tense Verbs	Future Tense Verbs
F			
R			
E			
N			
C			
H			

Affinity Diagrams

An affinity diagram is an organized classification chart that shows the results of a group brainstorming session. The purpose of this activity is to generate and classify information and ideas about a somewhat complex issue derived from content students study. Although the issue is complex, this activity can be used with all grade levels. The process is easy, visual, and based on collaborative thought. Table 4.1 is a lesson plan for how to use this organizer in the classroom. The lesson steps are located in Column 1, and an actual classroom example is described in Column 2.

Table 4.1: A Lesson Plan for Developing an Affinity Diagram

Lesson Step	Example
1. Pose a question or problem to the class.	Students are not eating nutritious lunches at school. There are healthy choices in the cafeteria, and parents pack healthy lunches, but students throw food away. What can we do to encourage students to eat healthy lunches?
2. Students brainstorm and record ideas on a sticky note or index card.	Ideas include more choices, longer lunch time, tasting days, special fruit and veggie dips, calorie charts, sample healthy snacks, parents packing better lunches, and giving prizes.
3. Students take turns reading their ideas and place them on a large piece of chart paper or on the table. While they do this, they are grouping ideas that are somewhat similar, explaining their thinking as they do so. Name each grouping with a title or heading.	The students come up with the following headings: a. Change the food b. Offer incentives c. Educate students d. Change the rules and schedules
4. Combine all ideas from the small groups into a class affinity chart.	One representative from each small group reads the category headings as the teacher labels those on a large class chart.
5. Discuss the categories and the ideas suggested. Value should be given to ideas that are similar or which were repeated often.	The categories suggest ideas for students to use as they solve the problem of encouraging students to eat healthy lunches.

Figure 4.4 displays the information collected by the students in Table 4.1.

Figure 4.4 Example of an Affinity Diagram: What Can We Do to Encourage Healthy Eating?

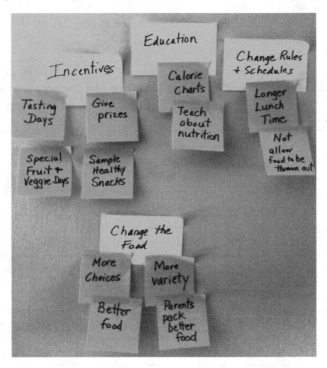

Dichotomous Key

A dichotomous key is a graphic organizer for classifying and identifying things—most often things in nature—using logical choices to separate them into various classes. It can be displayed in a flowchart format or as a simple chart. The dichotomous key is typically a set of two statements that describe characteristics of an unidentified tree, bird, fungus, or wildflower such as those found in field guides. Field-guide users have to choose which of the two statements best describes the unidentified flora or fauna they have encountered in their hike and then move on to the next pair of statements. Eventually, nature lovers are able to accurately identify the wildflower, bird, or unusual plant. The dichotomous key is particularly useful when comparing two things that are very similar to one another. This unique organizer is typically used with older students and frequently seen in science classrooms.

It can be used, however, for any subject when you want students to be able to identify an object as a part of a category—for instance, to identify a word as a particular part of speech or a composition as representative of a musical style. Students do not have to create an original dichotomous key to benefit from it, but the real benefit of creating one is a much deeper understanding of the content. After some experience reading a key, you may want to have your students create one. Table 4.2 is a lesson plan for modeling the creation of a dichotomous key.

Table 4.2: Lesson Plan for Modeling the Creation of a Dichotomous Key

Lesson Step	Explanation
1. Begin by explaining the term *dichotomous key*.	The term *dichotomous* describes two contradictory or totally different things. The key we create will help someone else identify something by a process of eliminating various characteristics. Figure 4.5 shows the completed key.
2. Select an everyday item to describe in your key.	The teacher has chosen buttons, giving each group of students six to ten of the same ones.
3. Determine whether you will use a flowchart or grid to display your key.	The teacher chooses a grid since it is more quickly constructed and students will be less distracted than by a flowchart.
4. Determine the most obvious feature or attribute that is consistent and easy to observe.	The students decide that the most obvious feature is the number of holes. They answer a question: Does the button have two holes or four holes?
5. Gradually move to more specific features, asking a question that has only two answers.	Then they answer a more specific question: Is the button made of metal or plastic?
6. Continue asking increasingly more specific questions until all of the questions are answered and each item is left alone.	Each succeeding branch states an increasingly more specific characteristic to classify the buttons until the distinct pathway of attributes points to only one kind of button. To check accuracy, show your students how to read the classification chart backward, starting at the end point and tracing a path of attributes back to the starting point.

Figure 4.5 is a sample dichotoomous key illustrating the process shown in Table 4.2.

Figure 4.5: Dichotomous Key for Buttons

1a. Button with two holes	1b. Button with four holes
2a. Metal button go to 3a 2b. Plastic button go to 3b	2a. Metal button go to 3a 2b. Plastic button go to 3b
3a. Metal button with two holes 3b. Plastic button with two holes	3a. Metal button with four holes 3b. Plastic button with four holes

Common Mistakes

Classification activities have application to almost every grade level and content, but effectively implementing this technique comes with its own set of common mistakes. Avoiding these mistakes will increase the probability that your implementation of classification activities will be effective.

- The teacher asks students to classify too many things at the same time.

- The teacher moves to complex content too quickly.

- The teacher fails to step back to let students develop their own classification schemes.

- The teacher fails to explicitly provide a purpose and strong connection to critical content so that students understand the "why" of classification.

- The teacher does not expect students to provide summary statements about how their learning has deepened through a specific classification activity.

Examples and Nonexamples of Implementing Classifying Using Graphic Organizers

Although these examples may be from a different grade level or content area than you teach, consider them as an opportunity to gain a fresh perspective or an alternative way of helping your students examine similarities and differences in critical content.

Elementary Example of Implementing Classifying Using Graphic Organizers

The specific learning targets being addressed in this example are *research cloud formations to identify weather patterns, learn that clouds can be used for real-time weather forecasting at an individual and local level,* and *gather cloud and temperature data to be used in creating graphs and reports* (National Oceanic and Atmospheric Administration, Standards Alignment to National Science Education Standards). The third-grade teacher is beginning to work on these learning targets and wants her students to become more aware of cloud formations they see in the sky. She develops two tools for her students to use as they learn how to classify clouds: a dichotomous key flow-chart (Figure 4.6) and a simplified dichotomous key in a chart format (Figure 4.7). She creates a set of PowerPoint slides that display single cloud formations of the four most common clouds: cumulus, cirrus, cumulonimbus, and stratus. She shows the PowerPoint presentation while leading students through the flowchart. Slide 1 is puffy and white. Where does that lead us? Slide 2 is not puffy. The teacher leads the students to keep making choices until they reach the point where they definitely know which type of cloud they are viewing. Since the students now have some basic knowledge about the appearance of clouds, the teacher makes the connection between the weather patterns associated with the different types of clouds. She wants students to create a dichotomous key that someone could use to do some simple weather forecasting. Students dig in to this assignment using their textbook and a variety of resource materials, both print and digital. The teacher is pleased to see that as students share their dichotomous keys, they have been able to make connections between cloud formations and the weather.

Figure 4.6: Dichotomous Key Flowchart for Clouds

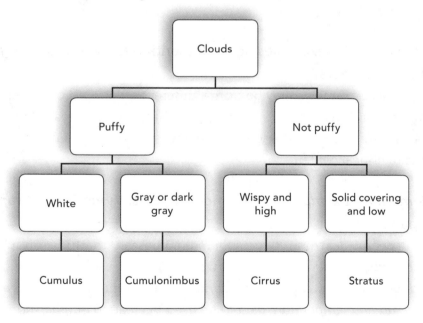

Figure 4.7: Dichotomous Key Chart Form

1a. Puffy cloud	1b. Not a puffy cloud
2a. Cloud is white go to 3a	2a. Wispy and high cloud go to 3a
2b. Cloud is gray or dark gray go to 3b	2b. Solid covering cloud that is low in the sky go to 3b
3a. Cumulus cloud	3a. Cirrus cloud
3b. Cumulonimbus cloud	3b. Stratus cloud

Elementary Nonexample of Using a Dichotomous Key to Classify Content

The nonexample teacher is using the same learning target but decides to wrap it all up into one nonstop lesson—classifying clouds and connecting them to weather patterns. He fails to model the process of constructing a dichotomous key and merely explains and directs students to construct one for using clouds to forecast weather. Students did not have a basic mastery of the various simple cloud formations and were not prepared to connect them to weather patterns. The students were not able to make connections and generalize about the various types of clouds and the weather.

Secondary Example of Classifying Using a Categories Chart

The specific learning target being addressed is *weighing the costs and benefits of different payment options when buying goods and services* (National Standards for Financial Literacy, Council for Economic Education; Standard II: Benchmarks 8.3 and 8.4). The eighth-grade economics teacher has taught a unit about what it means to be wise consumers. She and her students identified six different payment methods (shown in Figure 4.8) and are about to determine, by weighing the costs and benefits of each method, which methods are the best options for various kinds of purchases.

Figure 4.8: A Categories Chart for Classifying Expenditures

Cash	Check	Credit Card	Prepaid Card	Layaway	Rent-to-Own

Students worked in preassigned groups, and each group was given an envelope with index cards on which a typical purchase was written. The teacher asked students to categorize the purchases according to what they believed would be the best payment method. Examples of purchases were a ticket to a concert, food at a convenience store, an airline ticket, a cell phone bill, a beverage at a school basketball game, a car payment, living room furniture, and a bicycle.

Once their cards were all categorized, the teacher asked the students to note the similarities of items listed under each heading and note how those items differed from things listed in other columns. Finally, students were asked to generalize their findings by writing conclusive statements and recommendations about using different payment methods for different types of purchases.

Student generalizations included statements such as the following:

- Things that were consumed quickly or cost less than $10 were usually paid for with cash.

- Adults used a credit card to pay for purchases between $10 and $100.

- People put things on layaway if they were buying an expensive large item and could wait for it.

The teacher was generally pleased with the students' conclusions and used those as claims for students to examine in future lessons.

Secondary Nonexample of Classifying Using a Categorization Chart

A teacher down the hall was teaching financial literacy to eighth graders as well, with the same learning target as her colleague.

List all of the things you and your family members have purchased in the past two weeks. After you make your list, write the payment method used for each purchase next to the item. Then, exchange papers with your partner and create a new chart classifying your partner's purchases according to method of payment. When you are finished, return papers to each other, and see if you agree with your partner's categories. Count how many items were paid for in similar ways. For example, how many purchases were made with cash? How many with credit cards? We will report to the whole class and compile a class total for each method.

This classification activity, while having some merit at its core, did not result in students being able to describe similarities and differences among the payment options used for household purchases. In fact, the more the students worked on the task as assigned, the further away they actually got from the deeper understanding of the content. The students were not asked to make generalizations about the similarities and differences that they discovered, and few students came away with any depth of understanding of the goal.

Determining If Students Can Classify Using Graphic Organizers

Monitoring for the desired effect of this technique calls for you to determine if your students can identify similarities and differences in the content they are asked to examine. Many times, teachers as well as students get caught up in the excitement of an activity and forget to check for the intended outcome. Here are some ways that you can monitor your students' understanding of critical content as a result of using graphic organizers to classify it:

- Walk around the classroom, closely looking at students' work and listening in on student conversations as the groups work on the activity.

- Conduct a one-on-one oral or written formative assessment asking each student to tell what he or she noticed and learned while classifying using the various organizers.

- Students explain the reasons for their choices of various categories.

Table 4.3 contains a student proficiency scale for assessing how well your students are progressing from the beginning stages of being able to classify, up to innovating.

Table 4.3: Student Proficiency Scale for Classifying Using a Categorization Chart

Emerging	Fundamental	Desired Result
Students can explain a classification that was done by someone else. Students can determine some characteristics of the critical content related to classifying. Students can explain what they are classifying.	Students can determine appropriate categories using critical characteristics. Students summarize the results of their classification.	Students are able to explain the decisions they make while they classify. Students are able to explain how the classification relates to critical content.

Scaffold and Extend Instruction to Meet Students' Needs

There are many ways to scaffold and extend this classification technique.

Scaffolding

- Students can stay with sorting activities using concrete objects or pictures and words on cards as other students move on to more abstract classification charts.

- Present both the elements to be compared and the categories.

- Place struggling students in mixed-ability groups where they can be part of the discussion and contribute at the beginning of classifying activities.

Extending

- Expect students to choose their own categories, and include many different kinds of elements.

- Select certain students to be group leaders when creating affinity diagrams.

Instructional Technique 5

COMPARING BY CREATING METAPHORS AND SIMILES

A metaphor is a comparison between two things or ideas that do not seem generally related on a surface level but have a common pattern or theme on an abstract level. A simile compares two unlike things using the word *like* or *as*. A metaphor is generally thought to be a stronger comparison than a simile because the metaphor typically states or implies that the first thing is the second thing, whereas the simile communicates that it is only like the other thing (e.g., "Life *is* a journey" vs. "Life is *like* a journey"). Metaphors and similes are often paired as they are in this instructional technique. For younger students, similes would be introduced first, especially using sentence stems. However, when students have had experience with both of these types of figurative language, usually by middle school, metaphors or similes can be used, depending on the intended strength of the comparison.

Your students may have been taught to identify metaphors and similes in literature and poetry and learned how to create and use those figures of speech in their own descriptive writing. However, that is not the intent of this technique. It is designed to help you show students how to deepen their understanding of critical content through the creation of their own original similes and metaphors. To take your students to a new level of analysis and insight regarding some aspect of content, teach them to interpret, create, and use metaphors about important concepts within content areas. Wormeli (2009) calls metaphors "power tools" and suggests they can electrify learning.

However, creating similes and metaphors to deepen understanding of content is not as easy as turning on the switch of a power tool. Your students need several different skill sets to create strong metaphors and similes:

- a reasonable degree of content knowledge

- the ability to realize that they are missing some critical piece of information needed to create a suitable metaphor or simile

- the ability to locate the missing information as well as judge whether the source is trustworthy

- creative and abstract thinking to make connections between two things that seem quite different at first glance

- the ability to examine their own reasoning to test out their resulting work

- the ability to explain their reasoning to classmates and teachers

Once your students have mastered some basic critical content, explored the definitions, and watched you model how to create metaphors and similes, you will be amply rewarded by moments of sheer joy and brilliance. Think of the genius who came up with the conceptual metaphor "The computer is the new office" to teach people how to adapt to their new personal computers. The computer screen became the "desktop." We have "files" and "folders" and even "trash" and a "recycle bin." We adapted so quickly to this new paradigm because the strange was made familiar through the power of the metaphor. Once your students understand the power of metaphors and similes, they will be eager to display their creations.

How to Effectively Implement Metaphors and Similes

Metaphors and similes can help your students explain a complex concept by making connections between something familiar and something less known. Sometimes there is a familiar image that helps make the connection, such as the one in this simile: *Our country of immigrants is like a tossed salad.* Sometimes a concrete object or familiar action can anchor new information in long-term memory as the following metaphor does: *The senator hit a home run with his bill.* However, your success at implementing this technique is completely dependent on your students' foundational content knowledge.

The goal of this technique is to deepen that basic knowledge until it becomes part of students' long-term memories. There are several aspects of effectively implementing metaphors and similes: 1) directly teach and model how to create metaphors, 2) directly teach and model how to create similes, 3) use sentence stems and starter lists to create metaphors and similes, 4) use graphic organizers to create metaphors and similes, and 5) generate visual metaphors.

Directly Teach and Model How to Create Similes

Table 5.1 describes the steps to teaching your students how to understand and create similes. If students do not understand what similes are and do not have adequate practice completing and ultimately creating similes, they will be unable to take a big step up to creating metaphors.

Table 5.1: A Lesson Plan for Teaching and Modeling Similes

Lesson Step	Explanation
1. Introduce the vocabulary using student-friendly definitions.	A simile makes a comparison between two things that share similar characteristics. You can easily identify a simile because it contains the word *like*.
2. Present a simple, clear simile to teach a concept to students.	Choose examples from content if possible. Use a tangible object to help demonstrate a concept. For example, *our government is like the branches of a tree*.
3. Lead a general class discussion, asking students to make comparisons between the two elements of the simile.	Accept all reasonable answers, but ask students to explain their reasoning.
4. Lead students in listing attributes or important features of each element of the simile.	You might ask half the class to list attributes of one part of the simile (the government) and the other half of the class to list the attributes of the other part (tree branches).
5. Ask students to make further comparisons using the attributes listed.	As the list of comparisons grows, the simile will become stronger.

Once your students fully understand the concept of similes, you can begin transitioning them to the more powerful figure of speech called a metaphor. Table 5.2 is a lesson plan for directly teaching and modeling for your students how to create metaphors.

Directly Teach and Model How to Create Metaphors

The creation of metaphors is a challenging task for many students. Your first step in teaching how to create metaphors should be modeling and thinking aloud for students about how you create a metaphor. Two tools for helping your students create metaphors are sentence stems and starter lists. Note how the modeling lesson plan in Table 5.2 uses these tools to scaffold the creation of a metaphor. Column 1 contains the lesson steps, while Column 2 offers additional explanations and descriptions for each step.

Table 5.2: Lesson Plan for Modeling How to Create Metaphors Using Sentence Stems and Starter Lists

Lesson Step	Explanation and Description
1. Introduce the vocabulary using student-friendly definitions.	Remind students of the definition of a simile and explain the definition of a metaphor: an implied comparison. Also define the term *implied* (e.g., inferred, unstated, or unspoken) depending on the grade level and content.
2. Model creating a metaphor for students using a topic from content.	Parts of speech are familiar to older students as a topic for modeling. List the parts of speech as the categories of this topic. Then choose one part of speech: a conjunction.
3. Think of the attributes of conjunctions and list them for students as they come to your mind.	Conjunctions are short words, but they are essential. They connect series of words in sentences and clauses in sentences, and they get the readers from where they are to the next part of a list or sentence.
4. Once you have listed the attributes of conjunctions, use the starter list in Figure 5.1 to see if any of the words there compare similarly to a conjunction.	The category titled Things has some interesting words. The word *bridge* jumps right out as something that serves a similar function between two areas of land as a conjunction does between words and phrases.
5. Now that you have your metaphor, choose a sentence stem from Figure 5.2 to show your students how to write your metaphor in various ways.	Display the various examples to your students and think aloud about which one you prefer and why.

Figure 5.1: Starter Lists for Creating Metaphors and Similes

Actions: taking the temperature, taking a snapshot, opening the doors, walking a tightrope, playing tug-of-war, banging your head against the wall

Animals: octopus, chameleon, parasite, remora, fox, peacock, swan, ostrich

Business: Google, Enron, Edsel, Tupperware

Expressions: circle the wagons, cut from the same cloth, chip off the old block, rocket science, dust it off, baby steps, rose-colored glasses, balcony view, turning around a battleship, building an airplane while you're flying it

Nature: sunset, waning and waxing, food chain, birth, watershed

People: diamond in the rough, fairy godmother, king, clown

Proverbs: silver lining, rolling stone, new broom, ugly duckling, early bird, birds of a feather

Sports: hit a home run, close as in horseshoes, designated hitter

Things: monster, map, book, lens, anchor, ladder, umbrella, radar, circus, harness, bridge, thermometer, yardstick, dominoes, boomerangs, wake (water), dawn, heartbeat, cancer, security blanket, blinders, three-ring circus, mirror, fire hose, love letter

Time: December of our lives, era

Weather: sunny, icy, stormy, in a fog, cyclone

Figure 5.2: Example Sentence Stems for Creating Metaphors

Sentence Stem	Example
_____ is really a ___ _____.	A conjunction is really a bridge in my writing.
Think of a _____ as a _____.	Think of a conjunction as a bridge.
_____ reminds me of _____ because _____.	A conjunction reminds me of a bridge because they both connect important things.

Create Metaphors and Similes Using Graphic Organizers

Figure 5.3 displays a graphic organizer that can be used to help students analyze a metaphor or simile to better understand content. The example shown comes from a fourth-grade class that is learning about systems of the human body. The organizer enables students to elaborate on their metaphor in a structured fashion by providing two columns for describing how the elements of the metaphor are similar. The center column is for stating the common patterns or general themes that emerge from the comparison. The mere creation of a catchy metaphor is not your ultimate goal. Metaphors (and similes) are tools to help your students engage more completely with the content.

Figure 5.3: Creating Metaphors Using Graphic Organizers

Metaphor: *The human body is a house.*		
Element 1: *The human body*	**Common Patterns or Themes (Generalize)**	**Element 2:** *House*
Individual body tissues and organs work together in systems—for example, skeletal, nervous, and digestive.	Composed of systems	Individual things in a house work together in systems such as the structural, electrical, plumbing, and HVAC systems.
Body systems work together to keep people healthy and well. The nervous system depends on a healthy skeletal system to function as it should.	Systems are interdependent	Systems in a house depend on the efficient operation of other systems to run safely and smoothly. The HVAC system depends on a well-designed framework structure to contain and route the HVAC components.

Common Mistakes

The effective implementation of metaphors and similes is a complex undertaking, made even more so by the variety of common mistakes you can make:

- The teacher assumes that students have foundational knowledge of the familiar aspect of a metaphor or simile.

- The teacher lacks awareness of students' language and cultural backgrounds that can often make similes and metaphors incomprehensible.

- The teacher fails to engage in attribute listing in advance of generating similes and metaphors.

- The teacher fails to use objects, photos, and other manipulatives to assist with attribute listing.

- The teacher fails to appropriately correct errors students make when interpreting comparisons.

- The teacher fails to redirect students' faulty comparisons to an appropriate metaphor.

- The teacher generates too many complex or obscure metaphors.

- The teacher fails to understand the point of a metaphor: to bring clarity to a concept from critical content.

- The teacher confuses the identification and creation of figurative language in literature and poetry with using metaphors and similes to teach critical content.

Examples and Nonexamples of Creating Metaphors and Similes in the Classroom

Following are two examples (one elementary and one secondary) and their corresponding nonexamples of creating metaphors and similes. Note the ways that the example teachers demonstrate the effective implementation of this technique, and note how the nonexample teachers make some of the more common mistakes.

Elementary Example of Creating Metaphors and Similes

The specific learning target being addressed in this example is *explain the function of conjunctions, prepositions, and interjections . . . and their function in particular sentences* (CCSS English Language Arts Standard for Language L.5.1.a). The students in this fifth-grade class have learned to identify most parts of speech but are having difficulty with conjunctions. The teacher decides to use a simile to help students deepen their understanding about the function of conjunctions. She uses a direct approach and presents this simile sentence stem to her students: *A conjunction is like a bridge because* . . . She then gives students the following instructions:

> I have written a simile on the board: A conjunction is like a bridge. Your assignment is to discover why that simile is accurate. You have to find some ways to answer the "because" and tell me why a conjunction is like a bridge. *She has previously numbered her students 1s and 2s to enable her to give split assignments.* I want the 1s to list all of the characteristics (attributes) of conjunctions they can think of. I would like the 2s to use the Internet to scan photos of various kinds of bridges. The 1s should consult the anchor chart for examples of conjunctions and their uses in sentences. I'm going to give you fifteen minutes to complete these assignments, and then we'll combine what you've found to create a simile.

After identifying attributes and gathering pictures of bridges, the class came back together and shared their information. As a class, they contributed ideas to explain the simile and together decided the best response was that *a conjunction is like a bridge because it connects two parts of a sentence.* The students then summarized and concluded how the activity helped them better understand the purpose of conjunctions.

Elementary Nonexample of Creating Metaphors and Similes

The nonexample teacher selects a different learning target: *interpret figurative language, including similes and metaphors, in context* (CCSS English Language Arts Standard for Language L.5.5.a). Using metaphors and similes to help students understand various aspects of critical content is different from teaching these figures of speech in the context of reading literature and writing prose. Her lesson was strictly a language arts lesson on figurative language, and did not help students grapple with nuances in the content of the discipline. The goal of this technique is having students generate their own similes and metaphors. The first mistake the nonexample teacher made was in selecting a learning target that is incompatible with the desired result of the technique.

Examples and Nonexamples of Creating Metaphors and Similes in the Secondary Classroom

The following secondary example/nonexample is based on the following learning target: *Solve real-world and mathematical problems by writing and solving equations of the form $x + p = q$ and $px = q$ for cases in which p, q and x are all nonnegative rational numbers* (CCSS Mathematics Standard 6.EE.B.7).

Secondary Example of Creating Metaphors and Similes

A sixth-grade mathematics teacher is helping her students understand the use of letters to represent numerical values in equations. The lesson is focused on students learning to isolate the variable and solve by performing like operations on each side of the equation. To help students more deeply understand how to solve equations and expressions, the teacher uses a simile, comparing something new (an equation) with something familiar (a balance scale).

> Class, I am going to write a simile on the board. To review, a simile is a comparison between two unlike things using the word *like*. The simile we're going to work with today is: *An equation is really like a balance scale.* Here's an equation. *To help students visualize what she is talking about, she writes an equation example on the board, 2x + 3 = 25.* The equation is the first element of our simile. The second element is a balance scale. You no doubt have used these in a science class, but if you haven't, you need to take some time to experiment with weighing some apples using the scale and weights. *The teacher brings out a balance scale with a bag of apples and set of weights.*

The teacher monitors to be sure that students are familiar with equations in general and also understand how a balance scale works. They need this information to identify the similarities between the equation and balance scale. Students then use the graphic organizer displayed in Figure 5.4 to help them analyze the simile, working with a partner. After students work through the organizer, they write a summary of what they discovered about the similarities between an equation and a balance scale. Figure 5.4 shows how one pair of students completed the graphic organizer. Resource A.8 contains a reproducible template of this organizer.

Figure 5.4: Example of a Simile Using a Graphic Organizer

Simile: *An equation is like a balance scale.*		
Element 1: *Equation*	Common Patterns or Themes (Generalize)	Element 2: *Balance Scale*
Has a set of numbers and variables equal to something Example: $2x + 3 = 25$ $2x + 3 > 25$	Has two sides that can show equality (balance) or inequality (unbalanced)	Has two balance pans, each able to hold a separate weighted object
In an equation, the left side of the expression must equal the right side of the expression.	Each side must equal the other side to maintain balance.	The pans must each hold the same amount of weight to be balanced, or level.
To isolate the variable, apply an operation to one side and the exact thing to the other side (subtract 3 from left side, subtract 3 from right side).	If one side is changed, the other side must be changed for the sides to remain equal.	If the object, or weight, on the left is changed, the object or weight in the right balance pan must be changed for the scale to be balanced.

Secondary Nonexample of Creating Metaphors and Similes

The nonexample teacher also uses the simile to begin his lesson but approaches it somewhat differently from his colleague. He writes, "An equation is like a balance scale" on the board and passes out the graphic organizer. He directs students to immediately work quietly to fill in the attributes on the chart and decide on general themes. Some students understand the simile immediately, but a number of students ask, "What is a balance scale?" Those who do know are not familiar enough with equations to see any connections. The students are unable to generalize any deeper understanding of how to solve equations, and the activity is not a valuable learning experience. The teacher made the mistake of not checking to see if students were familiar with each component of the simile. To compare two things, students must be able to list attributes of each item, and then compare. The teacher did not provide a balance scale for students to see or manipulate, nor did the students have enough prior experience using variables. In addition, the teacher had students working alone, so there were no opportunities for students to share information or ideas.

Determining If Students Can Create Metaphors and Similes to Examine Similarities and Differences

To determine whether your students are gaining a deeper understanding of content through creating their own metaphors and similes, you must carefully monitor. Monitoring students' creation of similes and metaphors as related to acquiring a deeper understanding of critical content is almost as challenging as teaching and modeling the technique. Here are some ways you can monitor your students' abilities to create metaphors and similes that reveal similarities and differences in critical content.

- Students complete and explain a metaphor or simile that the teacher has presented to them.

- Students compile a list of attributes for both elements of a metaphor or simile prior to completing and explaining it.

- Students create a metaphor or simile using sentence stems and starter lists.

Use the student proficiency scale in Table 5.3 to assess your students' progress toward proficiency in creating metaphors and similes to examine similarities and differences in critical content.

Table 5.3: Student Proficiency Scale for Creating Metaphors and Similes to Examine Similarities and Differences

Emerging	Fundamental	Desired Result
Students can identify some important attributes of each element of a simile or metaphor but may also include some trivial attributes.	Students can accurately interpret a given metaphor and/or simile. Students can create an accurate content-related simile or metaphor. Students can successfully identify important content concepts in a metaphor or simile.	Students can create an accurate simile or metaphor that epitomizes the similarities and differences of critical content. Students can explain how a metaphor or simile relates to critical content.

Scaffold and Extend Instruction to Meet Students' Needs

As you become more skilled at teaching and modeling metaphors and similes as a way of deepening students' understanding of critical content, you will be able to more readily identify the students who need more assistance with this task as well as those students who are always one step ahead of you. The following suggestions are meant to be illustrative. Use them to inspire you to meet the precise needs of your students.

Scaffolding

Following are some ways to support struggling students in the use of this technique:

- Provide sentence stems or starter lists to help students begin their comparison.

- Use easier examples to help students understand the underlying concept of similes and metaphors before transitioning to more difficult critical content.

- Place struggling students in a group of four containing a range of student abilities in order to provide students with peer support and student models.

- Use structured graphic organizers to help students move in a step-by-step manner through the process of understanding or creating similes and metaphors.

Extending

Following are ways to develop an extra challenge for students who are more than ready to create advanced metaphors and similes:

- Encourage students to generate both topics and reference frames for comparison.

- Ask students to develop starter lists or continually add topics and objects to the current classroom list.

- Expect students to be on the lookout for metaphorical references in content readings and compile an ongoing collection.

- Expect students to point out instances in critical content where the creation of a metaphor would be appropriate.

Instructional Technique 6

COMPARING BY CREATING ANALOGIES

Analogies are a way of comparing the relationship between one pair of items to the relationship between a different pair. Use analogies with your students not only to teach and check vocabulary but also to help students deepen and practice their understanding of content. As they closely examine the items, deconstruct and complete the analogous sets, or create their own analogies, they will use the similarities and differences they discover to affirm and create new learning. You may have noted earlier that as your students were working on metaphors and similes, analogies often came up in discussions. There is a close connection between the two.

In fact, analogies can be thought of as a subgroup of metaphors. Both involve a close analysis of similarities and differences among words, numbers, and concepts, and both can be used to support claims or bring new clarity to content. As with previous techniques where students are examining similarities and differences, the amount of teacher direction can and should vary according to student knowledge and experience and complexity of content. At some point, you want your students to become so fluent in understanding and noticing analogous reasoning that they begin to use the method themselves as a way to explain or make meaning of a concept. However, you might want to begin by providing most of the information, and move your students from there in a gradual release of responsibility.

How to Effectively Implement Analogies

Using analogies to practice and deepen understanding of critical content will be most effective when students have already acquired some basic knowledge about the content. When you are confident that the majority of your students have basic content knowledge pertaining to a certain topic or unit, you are ready to effectively implement analogies. There are two aspects of effectively implementing the creation of analogies: 1) teach and model the basics of creating analogies and 2) create analogies using sentence stems.

Teach and Model the Basics of Creating Analogies

Table 6.1 is a plan for teaching your students the basics of creating analogies. The column on the left states your action as the teacher, while the column on the right further describes and explains the action. Remember that many of your students are accustomed to identifying analogies in literary texts. This is a more demanding process since it requires that students have a basic level of content knowledge.

Table 6.1: Lesson Plan for Teaching the Basics of Creating Analogies

Lesson Step	Description and Explanation
1. Prepare and present student-friendly definitions for the important terms and concepts needed to create analogies.	Analogy: a relationship between two sets of items Element: the individual concepts in an analogy Source: refers to the first, better-known set of concepts found in an analogy Target: refers to the second, lesser-known set of concepts found in an analogy Format: the various ways you can present analogies (See Figure 6.1 for an illustration of the most common formats.)
2. Present a simple analogy that contains familiar elements. Use this analogy to explain the various aspects of analogies.	*Sleeping Beauty :* fairy tale :: ice cream : dessert There are four elements in the above analogy. The first two are called the source, and the second two are called the target. They are presented in the Aristotelian format with a colon separating the elements and a double colon separating the source and target.
3. Explain to students that their assignment, as you begin to create content-based analogies, is to recognize the relationship between the first two things and apply that relationship in the same way to the second set of things.	Creating original analogies to represent critical content requires a substantial amount of background knowledge.
4. Present students with a partially completed analogy related to content such as the one in Column 2.	Canada : North America :: Morocco : _____

Table 6.1 *(continued)*

Lesson Step	Description and Explanation
5. Ask them to determine the relationship between the first two concepts. One way to scaffold this process is to have students create a sentence made up of the words in the first part of the analogy that explains the relationship: "Canada is a country on the continent of North America." They should then be able to use the same basic sentence for the second part of the analogy and just fill in the appropriate blanks: "Morocco is a country on the continent of Africa."	Even completing a partially completed analogy the teacher presents, such as the one shown in step 4, requires knowing the categories and critical attributes of the three geographical entities. (See Figure 6.2 for a set of common relationships found in analogies.)

There are four formats your students can use for creating analogies: 1) the cloze format, 2) the Aristotelian format, 3) the visual format, and 4) the graphic organizer. (See Figure 6.1.) The cloze format provides flexibility for you and your students. You can scaffold the process by filling in one or two blanks to create various sentence stems. Or, your students can use the cloze format to create an original analogy. The words serve to keep students' thinking on track. The Aristotelian format, as you may have guessed, gets its name from the Greek philosopher Aristotle. In this format, single and double colons are used in the places where words appear in the cloze format. The visual format is useful for using drawings or photos in each of a series of geometric shapes instead of the more common words. The graphic organizer shown is recommended by Hyerle (1996) as a way of depicting relationships in an analogy. Students are required to state the relationship between the two sets of items in a very specific way.

Figure 6.1: Formats for Creating Analogies

Description	Example
Cloze format	_____ is to _____ as _____ is to _____.
Aristotelian format	_____ : _____ : : _____ : _____
Visual format	☐ is to ☐ as △ is to △.
Graphic organizer	mammals / fish / monkey / Group and group member / carp
	Source: Adapted from Hyerle (1996).

Figure 6.2: Common Relationships Used in Analogies

Type of Relationship	Example	Sentences to Explain the Relationship and Test the Logic of the Analogy
Antonyms	offense : defense :: batter : pitcher	Offense is the opposite of defense. The batter stands opposite the pitcher.
Synonyms	promise : vow :: treaty : agreement	A promise is a vow. A treaty is an agreement.
Category/example	mammal : monkey :: fish : carp	An example of a mammal is a monkey. An example of a fish is a carp.
Example/category	*Sleeping Beauty* : fairy tale :: ice cream : dessert	Sleeping Beauty is an example of a fairy tale. Ice cream is an example of a dessert.
Class/ membership	metamorphic : marble :: igneous : basalt :: sedimentary : limestone	Metamorphic is a class of rocks of which marble is a member. Igneous is a class of rocks of which basalt is a member. Sedimentary is a class of rock of which limestone is a member.
Part/whole	fulcrum : lever :: hinge : door	A fulcrum is part of a lever. A hinge is part of a door.
Whole/part	city : neighborhood :: neighborhood : street	A city contains a neighborhood. A neighborhood contains a street.
Function/object	mason : stone :: carpenter : wood	A mason uses stone. A carpenter uses wood.
Agent/purpose	sunscreen : sunburn :: vaccine : flu	Sunscreen prevents sunburn. A vaccine prevents flu.
Quantitative/size	year : month :: month : day	A year is made up of months. A month is made up of days.
Cause/effect	rain : puddle :: nuclear reaction : radiation	Rain results in puddles. Nuclear reactions result in radiation.

Creating Analogies Using Sentence Stems

Sentence stems are one of the most effective ways to help your students create analogies. Table 6.2 displays a lesson plan for teaching students to create analogies using sentence stems.

Table 6.2: Lesson Plan for Creating Analogies Using Sentence Stems

Lesson Step	Description and Explanation
1. Create a sentence stem that suggests an analogy to students. Begin with an example that has only one element missing.	A cup is to a pint as a pint is to a _____. A sum is to an addition problem as a quotient is to a _____.
2. As students become more proficient at adding one missing element, challenge them with a sentence stem in which two elements are missing.	A cup is to a pint as a _____ is to a _____. A sum is to an addition problem as a _____ is to a _____.
3. The next challenge for students to tackle is an even more open-ended stem such as this one from an American history class.	FDR is to _____ as _____ is to _____.
4. This stem is taken from a financial literacy class.	Bankruptcy is to _____ as _____ is to _____.
5. Ask students to work together to complete the sentence stem using one or more of options 1–5 found in Column 2.	1. Complete the sentence stem orally, sharing with a partner or small group. 2. Complete the stem nonlinguistically by drawing, diagramming, or dramatizing. 3. Complete the stem first individually using text or notes, then comparing answers with small group. 4. As a group, consider all responses and combine them or choose the best one to share. 5. Complete the stem independently first, then consider text or notes to revise responses.
6. Discuss students' responses, noting what the various responses have in common or how they differ.	
7. Test out the logic in each analogy.	Is the analogy parallel? Is it valid? Does it add to the understanding of the content?

Common Mistakes

If you know ahead of time where problems might arise as you teach and model the creation of analogies, you will increase your likelihood of success in implementing this technique. Note the following common mistakes:

- The teacher assumes that students will automatically connect critical content to the task when asked to complete a partial analogy.

- The teacher accepts the first answer without encouraging students to think of multiple answers.

- The teacher does not require students to write complete sentences to show an accurate relationship when working with analogies.

- The teacher compares two ideas that are not really alike, resulting in weak analogies.

- The teacher does not model for students how to be sure that an analogy is completely parallel and the relationships shown are in the right order.

- The teacher fails to make students aware of the many possible ways the words might be related.

- The teacher lacks the content knowledge and pedagogical expertise to teach the necessary higher-level thinking skills.

- The teacher fails to present and consistently use student-friendly definitions for terms related to the creation of analogies.

- The teacher fails to directly teach and model the common relationships represented in analogies.

Examples and Nonexamples of Using Analogies to Examine Similarities and Differences

The following classroom examples and nonexamples demonstrate the use of analogies to examine similarities and differences.

Elementary Example of Analogies

The elementary example of using analogies to examine similarities and differences is based on the following learning target: *understanding the causes of the American Revolution, the ideas and interests involved in forging the revolutionary movement, and the reasons for the American victory* (National Center for History and the Schools History Standards: Revolution and the New Nation Era, Standard 1a). The fifth-grade teacher has spent the past week introducing his class to life in the American colonies leading up to the Revolutionary War.

Now, the teacher wants his students to determine some of the causes of the break between the colonies and England. To help them understand the content in more depth, he decides to use an analogy approach.

> By now, class, you have learned a great deal about the American colonies—the individuals who founded them, how they were founded, and their growing frustration with being ruled by the King. It might seem to us that it was an obvious thing for the colonists to break away from England, but let's see if we can dig a little deeper to understand the relationship between them. We may just discover that things were not as simple two hundred years ago as they might seem to us now.

The teacher begins his analogy lesson by guiding students to identify the actions, attitudes, and beliefs (attributes) of both England and the colonists. During this group work, he monitors students and redirects their thinking when it wanders. He then leads a whole-class discussion of the kind of relationship that existed between the two groups, and asks students, "What does the relationship between the two groups make you think of?" From there, he directs students to work in pairs to construct an analogy given the following frame: England is to the American colonies as _____ is to _____. Some students arrive at a parent/child relationship. Others compare it to an owner/pet relationship, and others think it's somewhat like a tetherball and post. As the class discusses the various possibilities further, they tweak the parent/child relationship gradually and agree on the analogy shown in Figure 6.4. The teacher brings closure to the lesson by asking students to help him write a short summary statement. He takes suggestions and works with the class in a back-and-forth way to come up with the statement in Figure 6.4.

Figure 6.4: Sample Graphic Organizer for Analogy—American History

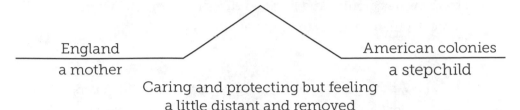

England | American colonies
a mother | a stepchild

Caring and protecting but feeling
a little distant and removed

Adapted from Hyerle (1996).

Elementary Nonexample of Using Analogies to Examine Similarities and Differences

The nonexample teacher is focused on the same learning target as the example teacher but approaches the topic in a different way. She begins the unit by having students read the six pages in their textbook about the American colonies and follows that with a two-day showing of the video, *Johnny Tremain*. The third day, she launches an analogy activity, presenting the students with an analogy to complete: England : colonies as _____ : _____.

> I would like you to work in your groups and brainstorm as many ways you can think of to complete this analogy. Try to think about what you know about England and the colonies and their relationship first, then go ahead and complete the analogy.

The attempts of students to create appropriate analogies disappointed the teacher. This is not surprising considering the common mistakes she made. Her students did not have a solid grasp of the content. She failed to take time to list attributes of England and the colonies and explain that the relationship aspects leading to the Revolution constituted the critical content. Finally, the teacher failed to adequately teach and model for students how to create analogies.

Secondary Example of Creating Analogies to Identify Similarities and Differences

The secondary example is based on the following learning target: *analyze how an author draws on and transforms source material in a specific work, e.g. how Shakespeare treats a theme. . . or how a later author draws on a play by Shakespeare* (CCSS English Language Arts Standard for Literacy RL.9–10).

A freshman English class has been reading Shakespeare all term and has foundational knowledge of the playwright and some of his works. The teacher wants to stimulate deeper thinking about Shakespeare's importance and influence in Elizabethan theatre. She wants students to consider previous works that became sources for him and also consider later works by others who drew from Shakespeare. To do this, she posed a couple sentence stems for her students that required them to make analogies. She asked them to complete the stems and be ready to explain their reasoning.

William Shakespeare was to Elizabethan theatre as _____ is to _____.

West Side Story is to *Romeo and Juliet* as _____ is to _____.

Students worked in groups and were asked to come up with several responses for each stem. They were given time for Internet research, which most did. Figure 6.5 displays several of the student responses along with the reasoning they used in creating the analogies.

Figure 6.5: Examples of Analogies Created by Students

Analogy	Reasoning
William Shakespeare was to Elizabethan theatre as George Clooney is to popular film.	Clooney takes historical events and makes hit movies based on the events. He, like Shakespeare was, is very popular.
William Shakespeare was to Elizabethan theatre as Jon Stewart is to current TV.	Stewart makes social issues humorous.
West Side Story is to *Romeo and Juliet* as *The Lion King* is to *Hamlet*.	Both *West Side Story* and *The Lion King* are Broadway plays based on Shakespeare's work.
West Side Story is to *Romeo and Juliet* as *Kiss Me Kate* is to *The Taming of the Shrew*.	Both *West Side Story* and *Kiss Me Kate* are Broadway plays based on Shakespeare's work.

Secondary Nonexample of Creating Analogies to Identify Similarities and Differences

The secondary nonexample teacher is working toward the same learning target as the example teacher. He gives his students a similar sentence stem to complete.

1. *West Side Story* is to *Romeo and Juliet* as _____ is to _____.

Because Shakespeare and theater are this teacher's area of expertise, he presents PowerPoint slides of popular movies derived from Shakespeare's plays. He locates film clips of ten movies and after showing each one tells students which of Shakespeare's works provided a basis for the film. Students are asked to take notes during the presentation. After the PowerPoint presentation is finished, the teacher directs students to complete the sentence stem choosing one of the movie clips they have just seen.

While this may have been an entertaining class, the teacher is the only one who worked. Students relied on the teacher's research and analysis to come up with the similarities and differences and were not required to do any rigorous thinking. This teacher could have added rigor to this assignment by giving students the responsibility for digging into the content.

Determining If Students Can Create Analogies to Examine Similarities and Differences

The desired effect for this technique is that students will be able to generate new or deeper insights about critical content as a result of creating analogies. This particular aspect of examining similarities and differences may well be the most challenging work you demand of your students. Close, ongoing monitoring is required. Here are some suggestions for monitoring whether your students have expanded their content knowledge.

- Students discuss their thoughts during the creation of an analogy as you walk around and listen.

- Students explain their reasoning about a specific element or complete analogy to the whole class.

- Students complete a graphic organizer independently and turn it in.

- Students explain how an analogy helps them understand and remember critical content.

- Students are able to create analogies from critical content.

- Students are able to navigate digital resources to find information needed to complete analogies.

Use the student proficiency scale in Table 6.3 to assess your students' progress toward proficiency in the creation of analogies to examine similarities and differences in critical content.

Table 6.3: Student Proficiency Scale for the Creation of Analogies to Examine Similarities and Differences

Emerging	Fundamental	Desired Result
Students are able to accurately complete an analogy related to content when given choices for the correct response. They are able to generally identify a relationship between the source elements, with prompting.	Students accurately interpret a given analogy related to content Students can explain how it helps them better understand the content.	Students are able to accurately interpret and create analogies when presented with important relationships existing within the content. Students can explain how the analogy helps them better understand the content. Students are able to interpret and create analogies when only the first set of elements is provided.

Scaffold and Extend Instruction to Meet Students' Needs

Scaffolding and extending for your students can provide mutually beneficial experiences for struggling students who need repeated exposures to the critical content and students who have knowledge to share with their classmates.

Scaffolding

- Break the learning of analogies into small steps, and in the beginning stay with the students through each step of the task.

- Provide easier analogies for students, based on simpler, but still important, concepts.

- Provide visuals or concrete objects to help make the meaning clear.

- Provide graphic organizers and work through the process with students, prompting them to explain their reasoning along the way so that you are clear on what they understand and know which gaps you will need to fill in.

Extending

- Provide differentiated analogies based on content for your students, having some challenging ones ready for students who show special aptitude.

- Ask students to create their own analogies, given only the content information and their experience with analogous relationships. Expect them to elaborate and explain how using the analogies contributed to their understanding.

Conclusion

The goal of this book is to enable teachers to become more effective in teaching content to their students. The beginning step, as you have learned in the preceding pages, is to become skilled at helping students *examine similarities and differences.*

To determine if this goal has been met, you will need to gather information from your students, as well as solicit feedback from your supervisor or colleagues, to find someone willing to embark on this learning journey with you. Engage in a meaningful self-reflection on your use of the strategy. If you acquire nothing else from this book, let it be the *importance of monitoring.* The tipping point in your level of expertise and your students' achievement is *monitoring.* Implementing this strategy well is not enough. Your goal is the desired result: evidence that your students have developed a deeper understanding of the content by examining similarities and differences.

To be most effective, view implementation as a three-step process:

1. Implement the strategy using your energy and creativity to adopt and adapt the various techniques in this guide.

2. Monitor for the desired result. In other words, while you are implementing the technique, determine whether that technique is effective with the students.

3. If, as a result of your monitoring, you realize that your instruction was not adequate for students to achieve the desired result, seek out ways to change and adapt.

Although you can certainly experience this guide and gain expertise independently, the process will be more beneficial if you read and work through its contents with colleagues.

Reflection and Discussion Questions

Use the following reflection and discussion questions during a team meeting or even as food for thought prior to a meeting with your coach, mentor, or supervisor:

1. How has your instruction changed as a result of reading and implementing the instructional techniques found in this book?

2. What ways have you found to modify and enhance the instructional techniques found in this book to scaffold and extend your instruction?

3. What was your biggest challenge, in terms of implementing the instructional strategy?

4. How would you describe the changes in your students' learning that have occurred as a result of implementing this instructional strategy?

5. What will you do to share what you have learned with colleagues at your grade level or in your department?

Resources

Reproducible Sentence Stem Template

_____ and _____ are alike

because they both _____

_____.

They are different because _____

_____

and _____

_____.

Reproducible Template for Venn Diagram

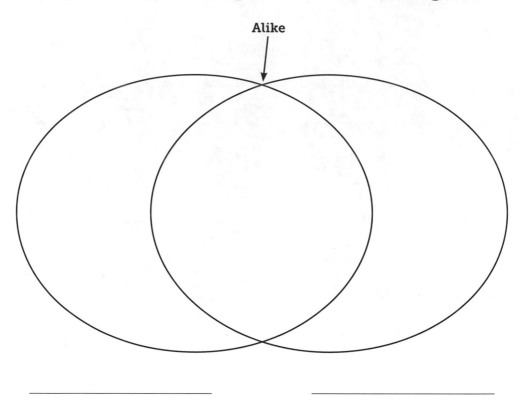

Alike

What I notice about the similarities and differences:

_____

_____

_____

_____

_____

Reproducible Triple Venn Diagram

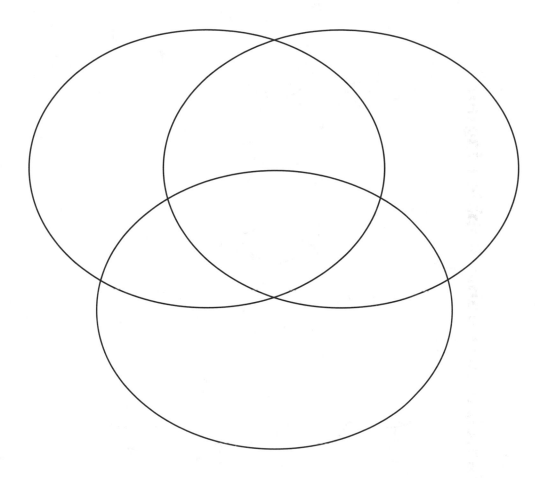

Reproducible Template for Double-Bubble Diagram

Reproducible Template for Comparison Matrix

Comparison Matrix for _____ & _____

Items to Compare ⟹				Similarities & Differences
Attribute 1				
Attribute 2				
Attribute 3				

Reproducible Template for Modified T-Chart

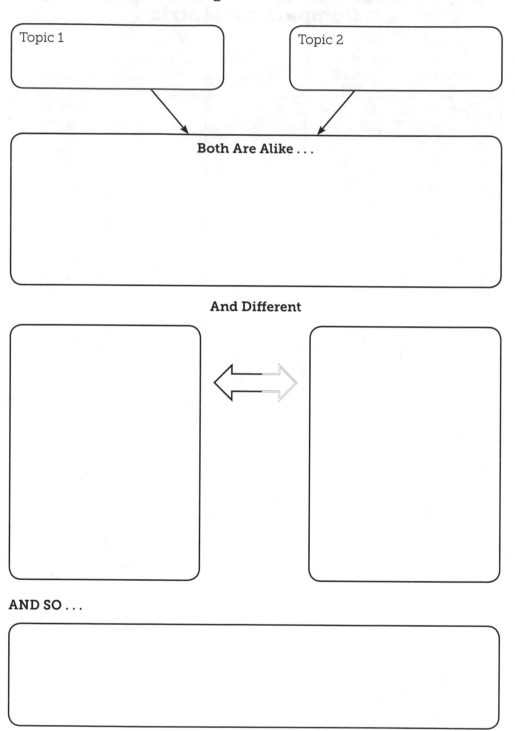

Topic 1

Topic 2

Both Are Alike . . .

And Different

AND SO . . .

Classification Chart

_____ Category 1	_____ Category 2	_____ Category 3

Planning Metaphors and Similes

Metaphor/Simile: _____		
_____ **Element 1**	**Common Patterns or Themes (Generalize)**	_____ **Element 2**

References

Achieve. (2014). *Next Generation Science Standards*. Retrieved November 25, 2014, from http://www.nextgenscience.org

Annenberg Learner. (2014). *Metaphorically speaking*. St. Louis, MO: Author. Retrieved November 25, 2014, from http://www.learner.org/workshops/nextmove/metaphor/

Bear, D. R., Invernizzi, M., Templeton, S., & Johnston, F. (2007). *Words their way*. Upper Saddle River, NJ: Pearson Prentice Hall.

Buell, J. (2012, July 10). Linking prior knowledge and new content with metaphors [Web log post]. *Inservice*. Retrieved November 25, 2014, from http://inservice .ascd.org/annual-conference/linking-prior-knowledge-and-new-content-with -metaphors/

Chapman, B. (2004, March 16). Conducting the activity. *Classroom Tools*. Retrieved November 25, 2014, from http://www.classroomtools.com/time_act.htm

Clutter, Ann W., & Zubieta, A. C. (2009). Understanding the Latino culture. *Fact Sheet: Family and Consumer Sciences*. The Ohio State University. Retrieved http:// ohioline.osu.edu/hyg-fact/5000/pdf/5237.pdf

Common Core State Standards Initiative. (2010a). *Common Core State Standards for English language arts and literacy in history/social studies, science, and technical subjects*. Retrieved November 25, 2014, from http://www.corestandards.org /ELA-Literacy/

Common Core State Standards Initiative. (2010b). *Common Core State Standards for mathematics*. Retrieved November 25, 2014, from http://www.corestandards .org/Math/

Dean, C., Hubbell, E., Pitler, H., & Stone, B. (2012) *Classroom instruction that works* (2nd ed). Alexandria, VA: Association for Supervision and Curriculum Development.

Dickson, S. V., Collins, V. L., Simmons, D. C., & Kame'enui, E. J. (1998). Metacognitive strategies: Instructional and curricular basics and implications. In D. C. Simmons & E. J. Kame'enui (Eds.), *What reading research tells us about children with diverse learning needs* (pp. 361–380). Hillsdale, NJ: Erlbaum.

Donn, M. (n.d.). What is figurative language? *Mr. Donn's Social Studies*. Retrieved November 25, 2014, from http://languagearts.mrdonn.org/figurative.html

Gess-Newsome, J., & Lederman, N. (1999). *Examining pedagogical content knowledge.* New York: Springer Science + Business.

Glynn, S. M. (1989). *Teaching with analogies.* Athens: University of Georgia. Retrieved November 25, 2014, from http://www.coe.uga.edu/twa/PDF /Glynn2008MakingScienceConceptsMeaningful.pdf

Hyerle, D. (1996). *Visual tools for constructing knowledge.* Alexandria, VA: Association for Supervision and Curriculum Development.

Illustrative Mathematics. (n.d.). *The IM mission statement.* Retrieved November 25, 2014, from https://www.illustrativemathematics.org

iObservation Resource Library. (2013a). *How to use analogies.* Blairsville, PA: Learning Sciences International. Retrieved November 25, 2014, from https://www .effectiveeducators.com

iObservation Resource Library. (2013b). *How to use classifying strategies.* Blairsville, PA: Learning Sciences International. Retrieved November 25, 2014, from https://www.effectiveeducators.com

iObservation Resource Library. (2013c). *How to use comparison strategies.* Blairsville, PA: Learning Sciences International. Retrieved November 25, 2014, from https://www.effectiveeducators.com

iObservation Resource Library. (2013d). *How to use metaphors and similes strategies.* Blairsville, PA: Learning Sciences International. Retrieved November 25, 2014, from https://www.effectiveeducators.com

Joyce, B., & Weil, M. (2004). *Models of teaching.* Englewood Cliffs, NJ: Pearson Education.

Lazar, G. (2004). *Exploring metaphors in the classroom.* London: Middlesex University. Retrieved November 25, 2014, from http://www.teachingenglish.org.uk /article/exploring-metaphors-classroom

Marzano, R. (2007). *Art and science of teaching.* Alexandria, VA: Association for Supervision and Curriculum Development.

Marzano, R., Norford, J., Paynter, D., Pickering, D., & Gaddy, B. (2001). *A handbook for classroom instruction that works.* Alexandria, VA: Association for Supervision and Curriculum Development.

Marzano, R., Roy, T., Heflebower, T., & Warrick, P. (2013). *Coaching Classroom Instruction* (2013) Bloomington, IN: Marzano Research Laboratory.

Marzano, R. J., & Toth, M. D. (2013). *Deliberate practice for deliberate growth: Teacher evaluation systems for continuous instructional improvement.* West Palm Beach, FL: Learning Sciences International.

National Council for the Social Studies. (2010). *National Curriculum Standards for social studies.* Retrieved November 25, 2014, from http://www.socialstudies.org /standards

Northrup, M. (2000). *Multicultural Cinderella stories.* Chicago: American Library Association. Retrieved November 25, 2014, from http://www.ala.org/offices /resources/multicultural

Ohio State University website. *Wonders of our World.* Retrieved November 25, 2014, from https://wow.osu.edu/experiments/Plants/Classification

PQ Systems. (1998). *Total quality tools for education (K–12)*, pp. 1–10. Miamisburg, OH: Productivity-Quality Systems, Inc.

Reuf, K. (1999). *The Private Eye (5X) Looking/Thinking by Analogy.* Retrieved November 25, 2014, from http://www.the-private-eye.com/html/abouttpe /Wht4_founders.html

Silver, H. F. (2010). *Compare & Contrast: Teaching Comparative Thinking to Strengthen Student Learning.* Alexandria, VA: Association for Supervision and Curriculum Development.

Source domain and target domain. (n.d.). Retrieved November 25, 2014, from http:// www.metaresolution.com/Metaphor/web_axonfiles/sourcetarget.htm

Tompkins, G. E. (1998). *50 literacy strategies.* Upper Saddle River, NJ: Merrill/Prentice Hall.

Wikimedia. (2014). *Caricature: Gillray plumpudding.* Retrieved November 25, 2014, from http://commons.wikimedia.org/wiki/File:Caricature_gillray _plumpudding.jpg

Word Sort Wizard. (n.d.). *Quality educational apps for the classroom.* Retrieved November 25, 2014, from http://www.wordsortwizard.com/

Wormeli, R. (2009). *Metaphors and analogies.* Portland, ME: Stenhouse.

Writing Center. (2014). *Fallacies.* University of North Carolina at Chapel Hill. Retrieved November 25, 2014, from http://writingcenter.unc.edu/handouts /fallacies/

Index

Notes

Notes

Notes

MARZANO CENTER

Essentials for Achieving Rigor SERIES

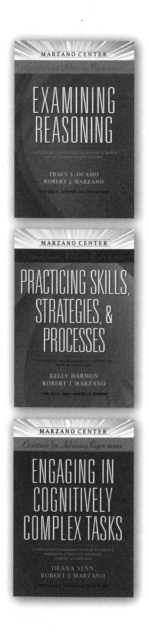

LearningSciencesInternational

LEARNING AND PERFORMANCE MANAGEMENT

Visit www.education-store.learningsciences.com or call 877-411-7114